"In *The Beginning of the Story*, Timothy read the Old Testament as followers on an experience of the Old Testament story of God culminating in Jesus Christ. Rich, scholarly, accessible, this book will deepen your knowledge of God revealed in Jesus Christ."

**DAVID FITCH**, Betty R. Lindner Chair of Evangelical Theology at Northern Seminary and author of *The Church of Us vs. Them*

"Irenic yet probing, Timothy J. Geddert masterfully uses the wisdom of a lifetime as a biblical theological exegete and scholar to unlock yet another puzzle: how the Christian reading of the Old Testament informs our reading of the New Testament. Engaging, insightful, thoughtful, and accessible, Tim writes for the church, seeking to draw together this often-polarized generation of Bible readers."

**LYNN JOST**, professor of preaching and Old Testament and director of the Center for Anabaptist Studies at Fresno Pacific Biblical Seminary

"Timothy J. Geddert's very readable introduction to the Old Testament is a must-read for followers of Jesus who want to ground their faith in the story that Scripture tells. While some Christians avoid the Old Testament or overly literalize it, Geddert guides us in seeing the continuity between the Old and New Testaments. The Old Testament records the up-and-down story of Israel, but more importantly, the Old Testament tells the story, albeit incomplete, of God, showing us a God at work with God's people. As Geddert points out, this is a work summed up in Jesus, who corrects and clarifies our picture of God. *The Beginning of the Story* convincingly reveals the Old Testament as the Spirit-inspired witness of God's work for us as the New Testament people of God made up of Jews and Gentiles."

**DEREK VREELAND**, pastor and author of *Centering Jesus*

"Timothy J. Geddert's conviction that the entire Old Testament is a 'grand narrative' of God's dealings with creation and especially the people chosen by God offers readers a compelling reason to reread these ancient texts and deepen our appreciation for the scriptures that Jesus knew and loved."

**VALERIE REMPEL**, director of accreditation for the Association of Theological Schools and former vice president and dean of Fresno Pacific Biblical Seminary at Fresno Pacific University

# the
# BEGINNING
## *of the*
# STORY

TIMOTHY J. GEDDERT

# the BEGINNING of the STORY

UNDERSTANDING THE OLD TESTAMENT
IN THE STORY OF SCRIPTURE

**HERALD PRESS**

Harrisonburg, Virginia

Herald Press
PO Box 866, Harrisonburg, Virginia 22803
www.HeraldPress.com

Study guides are available for many Herald Press titles at www.HeraldPress.com.

THE BEGINNING OF THE STORY
© 2023 by Herald Press, Harrisonburg, Virginia 22803. 800-245-7894.
    All rights reserved.
Library of Congress Cataloging in Publication Control Number: 2023021120
International Standard Book Number: 978-1-5138-1306-6 (paperback);
    978-1-5138-1307-3 (hardcover); 978-1-5138-1308-0 (ebook)
Printed in United States of America

This is a translated and revised version of a book originally published in German under the title *Das sogenannte Alte Testament: Warum wir nicht darauf verzichten können* (jointly authored by Timothy J. Geddert and Gertrud Geddert) and published by Neufeld Verlag, Schwarzenfeld, 2009, in cooperation with Bibellesebund, Marienheide. It has been translated into English and revised by Timothy J. Geddert.

27 26 25 24 23          10 9 8 7 6 5 4 3 2 1

*To my students*
   *. . . who have inspired me with their insights and questions,*
   *pushed me to be clear and persuasive,*
   *and joined me in discovering the treasures of Scripture.*

# CONTENTS

# FOREWORD

Read the Old Testament today? Maybe. But . . . proba-bly not.

I sit on my patio swing to spend time with Jesus, enjoying the warmth of the spring sun and the sight of neighbors walking their dogs along the path that borders our yard. Our back deck, when the weather finally warms up, is a space where heaven and earth almost seem to intersect. On this swing I quiet myself and seek Jesus with little agenda.

In this moment, I sense an invitation to read and reflect on the Scriptures.

*Perhaps I'll step into the Gospels.* I'm longing to engage relationally with Jesus, so why wouldn't I immerse myself in the stories that speak of his life?

*Or maybe it's time to read from the Epistles.* The more I read from Paul, Peter, and the other first-century writers, the more I discover the subversive and life-giving call to become human like Jesus, empowered by his Spirit.

Now, after a week of rushing between work, kid logistics, and the basic chaos of life, I bask in the sun's warmth, inhale fresh air, and pause to reflect on Jesus. Why complicate things by reading the Old Testament? After all, it lacks the Jesus-y appeal of the current moment.

Reading the New Testament helps me place Jesus at the center. This changes how I show up in ordinary life—how I love my family, treat my neighbors, serve in ministry, and beyond. I'd rather not spend the bit of quiet time that I've found in my week to read stories of conquest, dashing the heads of babies on rocks, and the like.

*So, read the Old Testament for once? It's been a while. Even if it doesn't all seem Christlike, maybe I should challenge myself and trust that it, too, is sacred scripture.*

*Hmm . . . I think I'll save it for the cold months.*

*On a sunny day like this, I'll read the Sermon on the Mount.*

❖

Have you ever had an internal monologue like this?

I'm a pastor trained in theology, biblical studies, and ancient history. I affirm the Hebrew Scriptures as *Scripture*. Yet I sometimes struggle to incorporate the First Testament into my regular spiritual practices.

This is where Timothy J. Geddert's book *The Beginning of the Story* gives us a framework to appreciate (and dare I say, love) the Old Testament. Like a wise guide, Geddert walks us through the full sweep of these thirty-nine ancient books. With a posture of empathy and invitation, he then addresses issues that easily trip us up—challenging portraits of God, the purpose of the law, acts of violence and warfare, and even miracles.

Geddert creatively demonstrates that the whole story is grounded in God's desire to offer healing and hope to the cosmos. God's strategy for bringing this mission to its future completion is through a *covenant*—or, to say it in a Jesus-y way that most of us "get," a *relationship*. The same God that we now know in Christ is the one who makes a covenant with the Old Testament people of God to invite them to live in such a way that other nations and peoples are drawn in.

Questions and frustrations are inevitable for thoughtful readers of the Old Testament. After reading Geddert's wise reflections, I see with greater clarity that these ancient stories offer the same thing I desire when I sit on my patio swing: a shalom-shaped relationship with our Creator. The God of the Torah, Prophets, and Psalms invites us to then extend God's covenantal love to others and the rest of creation.

As you read *The Beginning of the Story*, may you find that the "whole story" (from Genesis to Revelation) invites us to know Jesus more. May you be inspired afresh to read the Old Testament, and with fresh appreciation and perspective. I certainly am.

—Kurt Willems
lead pastor of Brentview Church in
Calgary and author of *Echoing Hope:
How the Humanity of Jesus Redeems
Our Pain* (KurtWillems.com)

# INTRODUCTION

There are lots of ways to read a book and lots of reasons to do so. I read some books for enjoyment, others for information, and still others to equip me in my Christian ministry. So, too, are there many ways to read the Bible—which is, after all, *a book*. Some read it mostly for personal inspiration; some mostly for ethical guidance; some mostly to gain insight into the nature and ways of God.

## READING THE OLD TESTAMENT AS FOLLOWERS OF JESUS

Those of us who confess that Jesus is the center of our faith read the New Testament to learn to know Jesus better—who he was and is, what he has done and continues to do for us, what he has promised to do when he comes to complete the work he began. This isn't the only reason we read the New Testament, but its relevance to our lives as Jesus people is clear. It's no surprise that many of us turn most often to the accounts of Jesus' life and teaching (the Gospels), to the stories of the development of the early church (Acts), and to the rest of the New Testament that addresses the life of the church and its mission.

But if we want to learn from Jesus and follow him in life, we must learn to read the first three-quarters of our Bible as Jesus did, and as the New Testament teaches us to do—for that collection of books which we often call the Old Testament was in fact Jesus' Bible and the Bible of the earliest Christians. It was of central importance to Jesus and the early Christian communities. When we read it as they did, it can't help but become of central importance to us as well, not only as a source of cute Sunday school stories but as a book that shapes our lives and identities as Jesus people.

In this book, we will explore what it means to read, interpret, and apply the Old Testament from a Christian point of view, following the model and directions given to us by Jesus and the New Testament.

The Old Testament can be read in other ways. Millions of people today consider the Hebrew Scriptures to be God's inspired word but are not following Jesus or seeking guidance from the New Testament. Obviously, they will read the Old Testament differently than I do, perhaps more like the people of God did before Jesus walked this earth.

Reading the Old Testament that way does not seem to me to be a valid option for followers of Jesus. We may well want to start there, asking what these ancient texts would have meant to the writers and readers of old, exploring how those texts were shaped and reshaped as they were read and passed on through the centuries, discerning how they were being interpreted and applied in different eras. All that seems like an appropriate way to start understanding these texts. But for Christians the task of interpreting and applying the Old Testament today is never properly finished until we ask, "How does the centrality of Jesus shape how we appropriate these texts today? How does the New Testament reinforce and illuminate, or sometimes relativize and transcend, what those ancient texts taught?"

This book sheds light on how Christians are invited by Jesus and the New Testament to read and apply the Old Testament. It is not a technical, academic book. Its aim is rather to model and inspire and occasionally evaluate, with the goal of helping us be enthusiastic and joy-filled readers of the first three-quarters of our Bible, guided by all that we have learned from the last quarter, the New Testament, and from Jesus himself most of all.

## READING FROM FRONT TO BACK AND BACK TO FRONT

Some people prefer to read books from front to back, others from back to front, and perhaps some pick and choose where to jump in and out. I smiled as I wrote that sentence, remembering how often I have discussed this very issue with my wife. She almost always turns to the last page first. I never do. To me it feels unfair to the authors if I don't let them draw me into the book and lead me along the way they have chosen. The intended effect is bypassed, the whole book spoiled, perhaps, if I know too soon how things will end. Besides, all the suspense is gone if I know the conclusion too soon, and without the suspense the book is only half as interesting. In any case, I put considerable thought into how I would begin this book, and I assume every other author does the same. Don't we owe it to an author to allow them to shape the way we start to read their book?

In my wife's view, we never owe authors anything. Her perspective is: It's my book and I can do with it what I want. I would never give someone else the right to tell me what to do with my books, what kind of experience I should have, in what order I should read the pages . . . backward, forward, diagonally.

My books; my rules! Besides, too much suspense diminishes the enjoyment of the reading experience, she believes. Despite years of trying to make our cases, we have not much influenced the other's reading habits.

What we do agree on is that the Bible is a special book. We agree that a great deal of what we read in the Bible remains baffling if we do not know how the story will end. Maybe the Bible should be read backward and forward . . . and over and over again.

## READING THE BIBLE AS A STORY

This is my most basic conviction about the Bible: It is a story. It tells a grand story, an epic story. Of course it contains many genres, but they all contribute to the story the Bible tells. If the Bible were merely a collection of doctrinal statements, it wouldn't really matter in what order the books of the Bible were read. We could simply find the appropriate verses supporting the topic of our theological study. If the Bible were merely a detailed account of ancient history, whether world history or salvation history, then we could flip back and forth as we studied whatever events were of interest to us. If the Bible were just a law code, we would merely need to find out which rules and prohibitions apply to our circumstances and needs. But the Bible is something else. It is a *story* from beginning to end, a suspenseful story about God and the world, about humans and the adventures they experience, about time and eternity.

The Bible makes numerous references to historical events in world history, and particularly to those events that most concerned a small people group in the ancient Near East and the relationship these people had with God and with their neighbors. And wherever the Bible speaks of these things, it does indeed become an important source of historical information. We are not reading fairy tales! But where historical claims are made, they are embedded within a story.

The Bible contains a great deal of theology; indeed it contains deeply theological reflections. But even these parts of the Bible are embedded within a story. And the Bible contains laws, commands, and prohibitions (and not only in the Old Testament). These are important to us as we seek to better understand who God is and who God calls us to be. But these are also part of a grand narrative—a narrative with high points and low points, with fascinating characters, with retrospection and foreshadowing. The Bible contains reports and prophecy, wise sayings and specific rules, worship songs and theological reflection. And these are all embedded within a story, the grand story of God's dealings with humanity, indeed, with the whole universe. The individual details don't mean as much without the context of the whole.

The story that the Bible tells is about a great journey. God has become our traveling companion on this journey, and God has determined the outcome. So while we read this story, we recognize that we are also characters in it. We, like the people we encounter on the pages, are travelers on this journey. In fact, as active characters we are even influencing the plot development. God, the main character and author, allows us an astonishing amount of freedom to participate in the development of the storyline. As a character with us in the story, God leads and guides, encourages and corrects. As the author of the whole narrative, God sometimes moves characters around and changes their roles. And God is always ready to show the way, to inspire renewed vision, and to reveal the best plan for us.

## READING THIS BOOK

Of my many goals for this book, this one is at the top: To help Jesus followers discover how a "Jesus centered" way of reading the Old Testament makes the whole story come alive. When we allow Jesus to teach us how to read the Old Testament, we will experience that the Bible is, from beginning to end (and even the other way around!), worth reading, fascinating, and of utmost importance. Without the Bible—the whole story of the Bible, which begins with the Old Testament—we would know almost nothing reliable about the one true God, we would be in the dark about the meaning and purpose of life, and we would stumble around trying to figure out how to get along with our fellow human beings. This encompasses fellow travelers on the journey with God, and those who have chosen other ways to live. But with the Bible, we have all we need to know God, to discover the true meaning and purpose of life, and to be guided along life's journey as followers of Jesus.

And this applies to the Old Testament just as much as to the New. When I talk about the beauty and meaning found in the Old Testament with other Christians, I often get reactions such as the following:

- But we live in "New Testament times;" the Old Testament does not apply to us anymore.
- That old part was just for the Jews anyway, wasn't it?
- Doesn't it contain mostly laws? We live in the time of grace.
- At most, the Old Testament tells us about a time of preparation for Jesus' coming. Now that Jesus has come, we live in the new covenant as we follow Jesus. Why should we pay any serious attention to the Old Testament?

Ever heard viewpoints like that? Well, I certainly would not have taken the time to write a whole book about the Old Testament if I believed any of that.

Even the name we have given the first three-quarters of the Bible, *Old* Testament, seems to suggest that it is not of much significance. It's "gotten old"; it's not relevant anymore; it's not *our* testament. I'm a New Testament professor by training, and when I teach graduate courses, they are mostly New Testament ones. But the more I try to understand the New Testament, the more convinced I become that the Old Testament is foundational to our Christian story. The Bible needs to be read both forward and backward. Without the Old Testament it is very difficult to read the New Testament—at least, to read it correctly. And when we read the Old Testament with eyes that have been trained by Jesus and guided by the New Testament, we learn just how important it is to the larger narrative we call the Bible.

As we embark on this journey together, there are some goals I hope to accomplish along the way:

- That you will rediscover (or perhaps discover for the first time) that the Bible is a fascinating narrative telling the amazing story that not only describes our lives but desires to transform them.
- That you will recognize that the Old Testament is a very significant part of the Christian story, and that it both enlightens the New Testament and is enlightened by it.
- That you will embrace what Jesus and the early Christian church knew: the pages of the Old Testament are loaded with indispensable guidance for the life of faith.

Each chapter deals with one or more important aspects of this grand narrative and how these individual topics addressed in the Old Testament fit into the larger story of the Scriptures. The first six chapters examine important themes from the first seventy chapters of the Bible. The Old Testament, however, contains 929 chapters (not counting deuterocanonical texts). Continuing at that deliberate pace, our journey through the Old Testament would be long indeed. However, the first seventy chapters of the Bible contribute a great deal to our understanding of the Old Testament (OT) message and help us understand both *how* and *why* to read the Old Testament.

The next four chapters consider the rest of the Old Testament. Chapter 7 includes a brief summary of the Old Testament and then focuses on a metaphor used in the prophetic writings: raising children. Chapters 8 and 9 openly admit that some OT topics cause great difficulty for readers. I freely admit that I do not always know what to do with some things written in the Old Testament. Since I assume these topics are also difficult for other readers, I attempt to shed a degree of light on them.

Of all the challenging topics, I doubt any are more important than the subject of God—portraits of God, claims about God, narratives of the sometimes inexplicable ways of God. Sometimes the ways of God seem questionable to us. The Old Testament contains wonderful pictures of God: God is a strong and gentle shepherd, a loving father, a careful vineyard owner. But what about texts where God seems to fly off the handle, command the unthinkable, and treat individuals in ways that seem patently unfair? What about those times when God's strategies for reaching goals include not only truth but also deception?

There are other difficult topics—like the pattern of repayment and retribution. Some texts seem to guarantee that everyone will get their just rewards: blessings for good behavior;

punishment for bad behavior. Other texts seem to argue the opposite, and so does human experience. It is at least as common in Scripture and in human experience that the wicked prosper and the righteous suffer.

Some readers of the Old Testament also struggle with miracle accounts. Did the miracles happen as reported, or did someone exaggerate the facts? I've heard one person argue that for all the Israelites to cross the Red Sea in one night, a three-mile-wide path would have been needed. Other readers stumble over how miracles seem to pervade the Bible while they pray in vain for anything similar to happen in their circumstances. Does God play favorites?

Then there is the ever difficult topic of war in the Old Testament. At times God appears to be a veritable warmonger, commanding terror and annihilation. And then there is the law. What are we supposed to do with all the laws that appear either irrelevant or inappropriate? Which laws are still valid? In what ways are they valid? For whom?

These questions deserve careful attention, and attentive readers deserve to have their own concerns about the Old Testament addressed. Can we really "salvage" the Old Testament in the face of such difficult questions? If not, how will we learn to understand and value the Old Testament? I will not shy away from the troubling parts of the story, the red-flag issues, the confusing topics. I will not claim to make things smooth and easy and logical. The Bible doesn't, so who am I to think I can? But I will try to build a bridge between the parts and the whole to help us live with what is unclear by seeing it in the larger context of what is clear.

Chapter 10, then, gives tips and suggestions on how best to appropriate different kinds of literature that we find in the Old Testament. What is the function of the Torah? What about those books we call "history books?" How do we treat the "writings" (that is, artistic literature)? What is our best approach to the prophetic books?

The final chapter explores how the New Testament continues the story begun in what we now call the Old Testament. When we learn to read the Old Testament from Jesus' perspective, we discover that one thing shines through every page of the story: God is faithful. If God were ever to become unfaithful to God's great plan, to creation itself, to God's people, to any individual—if God did not stand at our side and lead us along—then there would be no story to tell. The story would have ended in failure and destruction long before we could have come onto the stage. But God was faithful all through the story told in the Old Testament, demonstrating it most profoundly by "showing up" in Jesus. And God will never leave us alone, never abandon the great project that began with creation, until we celebrate the final chapters of this great story in God's presence, forever.

So now, knowing how this story ends, let's go back to the beginning.

# Questions for discussion

1.  How do you respond to the idea that the Bible is a narrative—not merely a theology book, a law book, or a history book?
2.  What are your first reactions to the idea that the Old Testament is not merely the book of another people group, but for Christians, is *our* book as well?
3.  In the Christian community with which you are most familiar, how is the Old Testament treated? Is it mostly ignored? Mostly disparaged? Mostly used for devotional reflection?
4.  What questions do you bring with you to a study of the meaning and relevance of the Old Testament? If you are studying this book with others, share these with your fellow travelers, and enjoy the journey as you keep reading!

# 1

# GOD, THE FAITHFUL CREATOR

### *(Genesis 1–2)*

*God created the world. —Mark 13:19*

*God made a man and a woman. —Mark 10:6 (CEV)*

There we have it: the most important things Jesus ever said about creation. Beyond these two statements, he referred to the act of creation described in Genesis almost exclusively as a time marker, pointing out things that have or haven't happened "since the creation of the world" (Matthew 13:35; Mark 13:19) or even before that (John 17:24).

Jesus never commented on most of the questions about creation that Christians debate today. Is the earth "young" or "old"? Are the creation accounts in the Old Testament mostly history and science, or mostly poetry and theology? What time frames and processes might be included in the Genesis 1:9 claim "And it was so"? For Jesus, the main thing remained the main thing: God created! We often argue about the details, but as far as we know, Jesus never made a single comment on these debated questions.

❖

"In the beginning God created." That is the first sentence in the Bible. That is how Scripture's story begins. Before God created, there was just God, God alone. If we consider what we learn much later in the story, then perhaps we should revise that: not God alone, but God as three in one. But God did not want to be "God alone" or even "God as three in one." So God created that which was other than God. But why?

There would be no explanation for this if God really were the kind of God that philosophers have often described. In humankind's attempts to understand God (or the gods), philosophers, theologians, indeed thinking people of all ages, have produced images of deities far too much like creatures to be the Creator—they may be stronger, or more holy, or less holy, but they seem too much like humans to be the creator of all. We want a god we can relate to, so we make God a lot like ourselves.

Sometimes we go to the other extreme. We start with a few characteristics of God found in the Scriptures—all-powerful (omnipotent), all-knowing (omniscient), everywhere present (omnipresent)—and then add other characteristics, like self-complete, self-satisfied, unchanging, immovable, unaffected, in perfect harmony, and self-sufficient. A deity is "defined" that is not only totally unlike humans, but also quite unlike the Bible's portrait of God.

The God of the Bible is not self-satisfied and self-sufficient. Most certainly the God of the Bible is not immovable, not in the sense that nothing can affect God, as Greek philosophers claimed. On the contrary, God had wishes and desires, goals in mind, and plans to achieve them. And so God created. God created that which was unlike God—the universe, nature, the earth, sun and moon, stars, living creatures of all kinds, and humanity. "God saw all that he had made, and it was very good" (Genesis 1:31).

Genesis 1 and 2 reveal to us that God is a creative God, and they spell out in considerable detail what God created. These chapters speak of the beginnings of all that is not God, the beginnings of the heavens and the earth. So let me be as clear about this as possible: Absolutely everything that exists, except for God, was created by God. The Scriptures make this affirmation from beginning to end. The entire universe came into being out of absolutely nothing, except for the powerful, creative Word of God. And it came into being because of God's intentions, not through some accident.

## PARSING THE DETAILS OF CREATION

Now, in terms of how God did that, all we learn is "And God said"! But in terms of why and for what purpose, the Bible gives us much more, especially as we learn to read the texts in their appropriate contexts.

Throughout the centuries, there has been considerable speculation about the *how*. Do Genesis 1 and 2 intend to set down the exact order in which each part of creation came into being? Do they indicate literal time frames when all this happened? Are we to take the six days of creation as literal days? As six epochs? As six aspects of creation? Or were they designed only as a literary framework for the narrative?

If God had wanted to bring the whole creation into being in a very short time, that would have been no problem at all, not for the God of heaven and earth. In principle at least, there is no problem with the view that God simply spoke and everything happened, just like that, all in six periods each twenty-four hours long. Yet many interpreters find considerable difficulty with this view, not in terms of the nature and power of God, but in terms of the content of the narrative itself. They ask, for example, how days and nights could be counted before there was a sun to rise and set.

Unfortunately, differing viewpoints on these questions have often led to bitter conflicts, with each side accusing the other of being either unthinking or unbiblical. And sometimes this has blinded us to what seem to be the far more important issues addressed in the Bible's first two chapters. If all our energies are expended comparing the Bible's account with the findings and the theories of scientific inquiry, we may well miss the main point.

Some will suggest that the whole question of time frames is an unnecessary conversation for those who follow Jesus. If Jesus is our authoritative guide for faith and life, then whatever Jesus believed about this is the final word. Case closed! But what exactly Jesus believed is hotly debated. For example, theologian Ekkehardt Mueller, whose goal is to defend a "young earth" interpretation, writes, "Obviously, according to Jesus the creation days were literal calendar days. A literal and close reading of Genesis 1 and 2 seems to be the proper approach to Scripture."[1] By contrast, the provocative scholar John Dominic Crossan writes, "My point, once again, is not that those ancient people told literal stories and we are now smart enough to take them symbolically, but that they told them symbolically and we are now dumb enough to take them literally."[2] And so the battle lines are set and jibes are often hurled back and forth.

What matters for us in Genesis 1 and 2 is that the universe and all it contains did not come into being by accident. It is the handiwork of creator God. And along with that comes an equally important point: God is not a distant deity, sitting back in the heavenlies, uninvolved, observing how the creation project unfolds. Rather, God is intimately involved, ready and eager to intervene and participate in the unfolding of a grand project that began with the creation of the heavens and the earth.

## GENESIS 1 AND 2 CHALLENGE ALTERNATIVE CREATION NARRATIVES

To understand the creation account in light of the larger story of Scripture, it is essential to examine the historical context in which Genesis 1 and 2 were written and in which they revealed God's plans and purposes to ancient Israel. The theological opponents of the ancient Israelites were *not* atheists building on Charles Darwin's claims in order to rule out the need for a creator God. Some interpreters seem to assume that, and then interpret Genesis 1 through this modern lens as though its protest were "No, no, no! The universe is not an accident; it is God's creation!" Nor were the opponents of the ancient Israelites scientists promoting the conviction that it took billions of years for creation as we now know it to develop. That is what other interpreters seem to assume. Through this similarly modern lens they then interpret Genesis 1 as though its protest were "No, no, no! You have your time frames all wrong!"

The theological opponents of the ancient Israelites were just as convinced as Israel that the universe came into being by the creative work of some god or gods. As far as we know, Israel never debated with its pagan neighbors how old the universe was. Nor do we have a record that Jesus ever weighed in on questions like this. These were not the questions they were considering. Israel's neighbors had creation accounts of their own, accounts that differed radically from what we read in the first chapters of Genesis.[3]

These alternative creation accounts were the focus of attention in Genesis 1. The real issues for the writers and original audience were, What sort of God (or gods) created the universe? And what paved the way for this to happen? Israel's pagan neighbors spoke of cosmic wars among the heavenly beings. Through murderous exploits and through triumph in battle, certain gods emerged victorious. They typically used body parts from their victims to lay the foundations of a world as violent as the heavenlies had been.

The Bible's creation narratives reject these claims. Through divine revelation, Moses and his followers countered such claims with the simple assertion: In the beginning, God had no opponents. God needed no war to emerge supreme. God needed no victims to lay the foundations of the earth. By implication, when murder and war did enter the picture, they came in as intruders, as perversions of God's good plan. They are not at the core of existence.

Some ancient creation myths spoke of great sea monsters slaughtered by the emerging hero. Genesis counters that even the creatures of the sea are part of God's good earth (1:21). Some ancient peoples worshiped the sun as a god. But Genesis counters with clarity that the sun, too, is God's creation (1:16). Some maintained that the influence of the stars determined the course of developments on earth. Genesis 1 counters this viewpoint with a matter-of-fact, almost throw-away comment: "He also made the stars" (1:16).

Again, the main point of the creation narratives in Genesis is that all creation is designed and brought about by the creative will and word of a God who desired it. At the beginning of creation, God had no eternal opponents; God needed no killing;

nothing in creation rivaled God's loving intentions or opposed God's creative initiative. No magic influenced the process, and no aspects of nature deserve our worship. All these emphases are introduced in Genesis 1, and then developed throughout Scripture and supremely in Jesus. How beautifully Scripture introduces a loving, generous God who created us to enjoy and care for God's good earth, our home! And how appropriate to respond with grateful hearts and joyful worship!

## CREATION SHAPES THE STORY

When we treat Genesis 1 and 2 as science per se, we miss the main points. And yet these two chapters ultimately lay the groundwork for all scientific investigation. We learn that the course of nature was willed and designed by God, then created by God and shared with humanity. We learn that God built into creation order and normal processes, what we have come to call the "laws of nature." Humanity was invited to enjoy creation and to seek to understand the "rules" that govern it. Giving names to animals (2:19–20) implies studying their very nature. God's commission to care for the garden implies that we are invited to live off the earth's bounty, but to do so in a way that protects and cares for it.

When we treat Genesis 1 and 2 as history per se, we also miss the main points. And yet these two chapters lay the groundwork for all of world history. Here we learn where it all began and its reasons for being. We learn that all of world history is within the loving, sovereign care of God. We learn that God has commissioned humanity to be coworkers. We are created in God's image so that we can be participants in the course of history, designed to fulfill God's original creative intentions.

To do justice to the first two chapters of the Bible, we need to look to the literary beauty of the narratives themselves. In the very structure of the creation story, we encounter a poetic form that gives meaning to the story it tells. The creation story is told in two parallel narratives: first Genesis 1:1–2:3, then 2:4–25. The first narrative is structured around six days when God created heaven and earth, heavenly bodies, land and sea, plants, animals, and humans. And God's assessment? "It's good! It's very good!" (1:4, 10, 12, 18, 21, 25, 31). And then God rested (2:1–3).

Then in a second narrative, certain details are brought back into focus and recounted in new ways. The special focus in this section is on the creation of Adam's partner Eve, a companion and equal to him. The first narrative emphasizes that with the arrival of humanity on the scene, God has reached the goal and sovereign purpose of the whole creative sequence. God is sovereign over creation, and creation gives God great pleasure. The second narrative emphasizes the role of humans in God's good earth, and above all the necessity of human community as the context where people can live up to their potential and fulfill their commission as God's coworkers.

When Jesus makes references to the creation narratives in Mark 10:6 and 13:9, he does not intend to weigh in on the questions of history and science that our modern minds have formed. Rather, he assumes the truth of everything that these creative narratives teach about the nature of God and God's relationship with and provision for human and non-human creation, truths shaped by very different questions from our own.

## DANGERS EXIST ON TWO SIDES

Perhaps we too quickly allow ourselves to develop a combat mentality between "Christians" and "scientists." The reality is that scientists, regardless of their religious beliefs, are far from unanimous in their conclusions about what processes led to the universe as we know it. Riddles and theories abound. Debates are energetic. Theologians are also far from united in their interpretations of Scripture on these matters. Some read Genesis 1 as literal science and history; others claim that it preserves the order of creation but not the time frames; others insist that Genesis 1 has nothing to do with *when* and *how*, but only with *why* and *by whom*. The lines are drawn, and each side is out to refute the other.

I see dangers on both ends of this spectrum. Our primary task should be to interpret the Bible, not to keep up with the newest theories in cosmology (a study of origins) and biology (the development of species). It is possible, after all, that God could create a universe, and humanity for that matter, fully formed, but with the *appearance* of age! If God can create a human who appears to be thirty years old, why not a universe that appears to be thirteen billion years old? Perhaps the greatest danger of adjusting our interpretations to fit the latest scientific theories is that we stop believing in a creator God. If science can explain enough to satisfy our curiosity, why not be content with that?

There is also a great risk on the other side. Well-intentioned Bible interpreters sometimes fail to distinguish between a justified confidence in Scripture and an unjustified confidence that we are interpreting it correctly. We are afraid to learn new things, lest our strongly held convictions be challenged. So we promote viewpoints that most thinking people consider completely impossible. Sometimes we need to relearn the "Galileo lesson."

During his lifetime, the scientist Galileo Galilei (1564–1642) experienced rejection (persecution, actually) at the hands of the Christian church for his newly gained discoveries about the motions of the planets. The church insisted that the Bible declares: The sun goes around the earth, not the other way around (as Galileo argued). Only when the evidence grew irrefutable (and the church began losing influence over thinking people) was the church finally able to admit that perhaps Galileo had been right. It took over 350 years for the church to formally state that it had been wrong in its treatment of what proved to be honest science. On October 31, 1992, Pope John Paul II finally issued an apology on behalf of the church for how it had treated Galileo and others like him.

While I respect Bible interpreters who in all sincerity are convinced the Bible teaches that the world is a mere six thousand (or so) years old, I also worry that they represent a church that needs to learn again the Galileo lesson. When I look through my telescope and observe star systems lying millions of light-years away, it certainly appears that God created all this across vast expanses of space and time, not all at once about six thousand years ago. And when other interpreters respond, "God simply created everything with the appearance of age," I respond, "Yes, God could have done that. But that does not seem to be the way God normally works."[4]

We need more than telescopes and microscopes and more than geology and the fossil record to reach well-founded conclusions on the real origins of the universe. Christians rely on the revealed Word of God to speak the final word. I plead for us to trust the written record, and to be genuinely humble about our ability to determine exactly what it says. If we read it with only our own burning questions in mind and ignore the issues that the original authors were addressing, we just might be misreading the texts just as we now know the church was doing in Galileo's day.

## CREATION REVEALS OUR ROLE IN THE LARGER STORY

All this leaves us quite divided, unfortunately. Some who defend a "young earth theory" (many would also call them "creationists") are prepared to argue that the earth is only a few thousand years old and that every appearance to the contrary was built into the original creation. Stars may well be millions of light-years away, but God created them with their light already having traveled all the way to us. Rocks may contain fossils that give the impression that the earth has been reshaped over many millions of years, but God simply created it with that appearance (or perhaps a cataclysmic early flood produced all those impressions).

Others consider it quite unnecessary to defend the idea of a young earth. Some embrace the concept of "intelligent design," proposing that God either actively guided or predetermined in detail the virtually infinite number of steps that led to the development of the universe as we know it. Others leave the question far more open than that. They insist: God is the ultimate Creator. Through what mechanisms and in what time frames God has been creatively at work is not the concern of the biblical narratives. Let's let the scientists among us work that one out as best they can while the rest of us hold fast to the primary conviction that God is the sovereign Lord of heaven and earth and we are stewards of God's good earth.

The final word in this discussion has not been spoken, and undoubtedly the debate will continue. But the first word in it stands firm: "In the beginning God created." And that is pretty much the only thing that Jesus ever said about creation. Jesus intended for his followers to focus on acknowledging God as a loving and faithful Creator rather than on debatable questions about how God did it. "In the beginning God created" sets the stage for the story of Scripture, the story of God, and all that

God created. God had plans and purposes. God became creative. God brought into being all of creation, with humanity as God's crowning achievement. God endowed humanity with the ability to be creative and gave us freedom to choose how it would be exercised. God made us stewards of creation and thus coworkers in shaping the course of history. God's own goals and purposes, though we may grasp them only in part, stand firm.

How does this transform our lives? We can be assured God will never abandon this world and its creatures (and especially will not abandon us humans) simply to our own devices. God's ingenious, creative faithfulness will somehow be sufficient to lead all of creation to its God-intended goal, even though God has intended for us to help shape history. In a real sense, God has shared divine power and prerogatives with us. And as we will explore in the next chapter, God does not normally intervene the instant we misuse that power and privilege.

In addition to all that the creation narratives tell us about how and why God created, they also tell us a great deal about our role in this grand story. So we will turn toward what these first chapters of Genesis tell us about how and why God created *us*. As we examine God's instructions to Adam and Eve, we see how these narratives also shape and give meaning to our lives and our role in the ongoing story of God and creation.

## GENESIS REPORTS THE FIRST INSTRUCTIONS FOR HUMANS

*Be fruitful and increase in number*

As Genesis tells the story, God filled the heavens with birds, the sea with fish, and the land with animals. The whole earth was teeming with life! But God did not fill the earth with humans. God created Adam and Eve and told *them* to fill it. "God blessed them and said to them, 'Be fruitful and increase in number; fill the earth . . .'" (Genesis 1:28). Perhaps this is the only command of God that humanity has truly succeeded in obeying.

Every time a child is conceived, God is creating anew. But God is choosing to do so in partnership with humanity, stewards of God's creation and participants in God's creative work. And every child born into this world is created in the image of God, just as Adam and Eve were (1:26–27). God brought Adam and Eve into the world to participate in God's project. We bring children into the world and invite them to join us in doing the same. What a privilege, and what a responsibility!

### Subdue and rule

God's good earth had not yet reached its full potential when humanity entered the scene. Perhaps we should say the universe was innocent but not yet mature, sinless but not yet perfected, very good but not yet at the goal. God created the earth and humans with great potential. God intended to lead humans along a journey to the consummation of God's plans. And God would always remain true to God's creation, even if the creation should in all sorts of ways turn its back on God.

And indeed we did, and do. First Peter 4:19 tells us, "So then, those who suffer according to God's will should commit themselves to their faithful Creator and continue to do good." This identification of God as a "faithful Creator" appears only once in all of Scripture, and in a context acknowledging that life comprises more than what is beautiful and wonderful. There is also pain and suffering. Indeed, a great deal of the suffering is a direct consequence of God's creation not remaining faithful to its faithful Creator.

Paul argues in Romans that unless and until God leads *humanity* to its full potential, creation itself will not reach the goals God has for it (8:18–21). So right from the start, God commissioned the first humans with these words: "Be fruitful and increase in number; fill the earth and *subdue* it. *Rule* over the fish in the sea and the birds in the sky and over every living creature that moves on the ground" (Genesis 1:28, emphasis added). Because the italicized words are often misinterpreted and then seriously misapplied, because humans are often inclined to abuse and misuse, this commission deserves a closer examination.

*Rule* (*radah* in Hebrew) is often understood to mean "suppress" or "domineer over." The Hebrew word can mean that, but usually does so in contexts where the "ruling" is connected to violence or to selfish personal gain. But when *rule* (that is, *radah*) is accomplished in accordance with God's will and purpose, then it is to be understood as "superintending." The texts often say, "Do not rule over them ruthlessly, but fear your God" (for example, Leviticus 25:43, 46, 53).

*Rule* implies practicing justice and mercy, offering help and protection, creating shalom. If it is necessary to rule by force, that force is to be employed to stop violence and abuse, to sustain or create just and peaceful relationships (see Psalm 72).

When we exploit the treasures of the earth for personal satisfaction, when we ignore or violate the fragile parts of creation, when we misuse power, when we block justice instead of creating it, then we have completely misunderstood what God meant by "rule over creation."

When we understand *rule* rightly, then we can also understand what God meant with the other command in Genesis 1:28: *subdue* (*kabash*). We are to subdue everything that is working against God's intended shalom. Our commission is to tear down the walls that hinder just relationships; it is to invest our best energies in stopping those who oppress the powerless;

it is to withdraw support of those systems and behavior patterns that pull God's creation out of the good paths God has designed for it.

Humanity—Adam and Eve first, then their descendants, now you and me—is the crown of God's creation. We are participants in the unfolding of history; we are God's assistants. God's goals for creation must be our goals for it as well. Through love and care, through insightful attention and selfless personal sacrifice, we watch out that nothing and nobody falls between the cracks. We lead and serve so that all of God's creation can find the shalom that God intended.

## CREATION ACCOUNTS HIGHLIGHT HUMAN DIGNITY

Several times already I have used the word *shalom* as if it were an ordinary English word. In fact, even in the original Hebrew it is not an ordinary word; it is a very special word. It is the word used to describe a condition where all is as it should be, all relationships healthy, all needs met, where nobody owes anybody anything. Shalom is a dream and a goal. The creation stories of Genesis 1 and 2 describe a world experiencing shalom.

And then came the fall. The consequences were horrendous; shalom was shattered. But God's image in humanity was not removed or destroyed. Even after the fall, humanity remained the crown of God's creation, even when they began to "subdue and rule" with little concern for justice. Yes, the first human pair ate the forbidden fruit and changed everything. But that did not change our deepest nature, our place in God's creation, and our commission from God.

I used to see that quite differently. But over forty years ago, while I was a seminary student, I experienced something unforgettable in an Old Testament theology class. It completely changed my understanding of how God sees us, and how God sees me. I remember the details to this day.

Our professor suggested, playfully I suppose, that we engage in an exercise. We were to create a scale numbered one through ten and place the various aspects of God's creation at appropriate places on that scale. The lowest creature would be considered a one, and naturally ten was reserved for the creator God—that is, no creature could be placed at the top of the scale. (After all, the highest honor must always belong to God.) I think the professor deliberately avoided using zero, for the lowest creatures are still creations of God. I remember our class debating which creature we'd place at the bottom of the scale—snakes? cockroaches? worms, perhaps? We had fun evaluating all creatures great and small, though we disagreed about most of the placements.

After a minute or two came the crucial question: "And where on the scale would you place humans?" My friend (of a different theological persuasion than me) shot forth an immediate answer: "One and a quarter . . . at the most!" Others immediately contradicted him. "At least five!" Someone dared to propose, "How about seven?" After playing with numbers a while, our professor asked, "Why don't we check out a text in the Bible where the question is both asked and answered? Please turn in your Bibles to Psalm 8."

I knew the psalm quite well, having memorized it earlier in Bible school. "LORD, our Lord, how majestic is your name in all the earth!" (8:1). There we have it: God is a ten! The psalm continues with assurances that no enemy can dethrone God's position; that even children and infants can affirm it! "Through the praise of children and infants you have established a stronghold against your enemies, to silence the foe and the avenger" (8:2).

And then the psalmist asks the central questions: "When I consider your heavens, the work of your fingers, the moon and the stars, which you have set in place, what is mankind that you are mindful of them, human beings that you care for them?" (8:3–4). That was the very question I had so often asked as a young child, especially on clear winter nights. Growing up in the far north, we often skated round and round our open-air ice rink, lights switched off, fascinated by millions of stars that made up the Milky Way, Northern Lights often dancing alongside.

I felt very small! If I didn't ask the question, I felt it: *When I consider your heavens . . . what is mankind that you are mindful of them, human beings that you care for them?* The huge expanse of the universe made me feel so small, so insignificant. Did God even notice me? Am I perhaps really a one and a quarter among all these glorious sevens and eights and nines?

My feelings echoed what I read in other biblical texts, like "Lord, what are human beings that you care for them, mere mortals that you think of them? They are like a breath; their days are like a fleeting shadow" (Psalm 144:3–4), and "The life of mortals is like grass, they flourish like a flower of the field; the wind blows over it and it is gone, and its place remembers it no more" (Psalm 103:15–16). The fragility, the dependence, the transience of our human condition seemed evidence to me that we don't play a very significant part in God's great plan for creation. So I read Psalm 8 from that perspective.

For me, the psalmist's question was, "God, do you pay attention at all to such tiny insignificant creatures as us, given the magnificence of those parts of your creation with so much glory?" Not for my professor. After hearing our musings, he turned everything upside down. He asked, "Why don't we just read Psalm 8:3–4 as a genuine question, not an expression of an inferiority complex, and then read verse 5 as God's answer?" Here is verse 5: "You have made them a little lower than God and crowned them with glory and honor" (NRSVue and similarly all other literal translations of this verse).

Doesn't that mean, our professor continued, that we should consider ourselves at least an eight, or perhaps a nine? If that doesn't seem to leave enough room for the glorious parts of creation the psalmist has already mentioned (the heavens, the moon, the stars), no problem. We'll just give them a lower number! "You made them [humans] rulers over the works of your hands [moon, stars!]; you put everything under their feet" (8:6). More glorious than the Milky Way! More honored than the Northern Lights! That is how God sees us and invites us to see ourselves. And when the psalmist goes on to name flocks and herds, birds and fish (8:7–8), this is a rerun of the creation mandate in Genesis 1. Humanity is the crown of creation, and remains that, even after the fall! We could almost call ourselves a ten, but to do so would be to repeat the fall, yielding to the temptation to try to be like God. So the psalmist warns us: No, ten is reserved for God! "LORD, our Lord, how majestic is your name in all the earth!" (8:9). The psalm ends as it begins.

We are all a nine, or perhaps a nine and a half—even after the fall. The fall of humanity makes it harder to carry out our commission, but it does not change the assignment. We remain the crown of God's creation. Our assignment is still to subdue and rule. We subdue by working for justice. We rule by protecting the fragile and the endangered. We join God's mission to preserve shalom where it exists and re-create it where it has disappeared. Our creation mandate is exactly what it has always been.

What happened when Adam and Eve were not content to be a nine and wanted to be a ten like God? That is what we call "the fall," which we explore in the next chapter.

## WHY IS IT IMPORTANT TO STUDY THE CREATION NARRATIVES?

"We are New Testament Christians," I sometimes hear. "Why should we bother reading the Old Testament?" The first answer among many could be formulated like this: Without the Old Testament we would have only a sketchy awareness of the first and most central commission God ever gave us: to be caretakers of creation and participants with God in shaping world history. The story of creation comes to us through the OT people of God, the Israelites. But it is the story of all humanity and of the one faithful God, creator of heaven and earth. That makes Genesis 1 and 2 among the most important chapters in the entire Bible, and a powerful beginning of the story.

# Questions for discussion

1.  Discuss the idea that the creation narratives of Scripture are more concerned with the nature of creator God and God's relationship with the creation than with the sequence of events and the time frames of creation.

2.  What do you think "subdue and rule" means? What does it mean to you in your daily life? Perhaps it would be helpful to compare different Bible translations of Genesis 1:28. How can we as individual followers of Jesus and as Christian communities contribute to this "creation mandate"?

3.  "More glorious than the Milky Way! More honored than the Northern Lights! That is how God sees us and invites us to see ourselves." If this is true, what are the implications for our self-perceptions and for our relationships with other people?

# GOD, THE ULTIMATE VICTOR

*(Genesis 3–11)*

*I saw Satan fall like lightning from heaven. —Luke 10:18*

Was Jesus reporting a prehistoric event in the heavenlies when one of God's archangels rebelled and was cast out of the heavenly council? Was Jesus looking forward to the coming victory at the end of time when God's archenemy will be fully and finally defeated? The context of Jesus' declaration was the missionary engagement of his first followers, so was he seeing a real, but not yet ultimate, victory over God's supernatural enemy? Perhaps it was all of the above. To glimpse God's long-range strategy to gain the final victory over the powers of evil, we need to examine what Genesis reports all too quickly after God pronounced creation good, indeed very good.

❖

"We have met the enemy, and he is us!" So goes the famous saying from Pogo, a fictional character created by American cartoonist Walter Kelly. Often, we really are our own worst enemies, which we see demonstrated in Genesis 3–11. The first two chapters already hinted that there would be trouble ahead. Why else would there be a need to subdue and rule?

The beginning of Genesis 3 adds hints to answer the question. The command not to eat of the tree of knowledge of good and evil implies that human obedience is not something that can be counted on. Humans will need to make choices. And where right choices are possible, so are wrong ones.

## DECEPTION BY THE SNAKE

Genesis 3 reports the temptation that Adam and Eve faced. The serpent's strategy was to make them insecure about what God had said, and what God had meant. "Are you sure God has your best interests at heart? Does God perhaps want to withhold something good from you?" The tempting voice proposed that the first human pair would be disadvantaging themselves if they obeyed God's instructions. After all, the forbidden fruit seemed perfect, beautiful, desirable. "God just wants to control your every movement, wants to prescribe exactly what you should and shouldn't do. A decision against God's will would be a step toward freedom, toward self-actualization."

The serpent twists the truth. It's true that God wants humans to decide for themselves, and that involves a degree of self-determination. Even though God made it *possible* for humans to act counter to God's expressed will, that was never God's intention. God took a risk, and the worst possible outcome happened. Humanity made a basic choice: We will go our own way. Satan had spoken enticing words; but Adam and Eve made the disastrous choice.

As soon as the first human pair took that giant leap into self-determination, it turned out so different from what they had anticipated, so different from what the snake had promised. They were supposed to become like God, but the first consequences didn't look very promising. Until now they had lived in harmony with both creator God and creation. Now this harmony was seriously marred. God sought their company, but they felt afraid and compelled to hide from God (3:8–9). The man blamed the woman; the woman blamed the snake. And both Adam and Eve felt ashamed (3:7, 11–12).

Soon after, we learn that God's commission to populate the earth could be fulfilled only through pain and suffering—that God's commission to care for the garden could be fulfilled only through toil and sweat (3:16–19). Conflict between the offspring of the woman and the serpent is predicted, a conflict that will turn out to be a main theme of Scripture. Humans still lived on the very same good earth, God's creation. But it had become a theater of war in the great battle between good and evil.

We often imagine that the battle line runs between people, between people groups, between religions, perhaps. However, the battle line runs straight through the heart of every human being. We have divided hearts and need God's intervention to become whole again. That is true not only for every individual; it is also true for families and societies. "We have met the enemy, and he is us!"

An enemy of God was speaking through the serpent. But from where did this enemy of God come? The best theological minds have wrestled with this question. The whole matter of "good and evil" needs to take seriously the following important claims:

- Only God has existed from all eternity. All else came into being by God's creative act. Whatever evil ultimately is, it came into being somewhere along the way, and thus has no ultimate eternal right to be here.

- God is good, only good! Evil is not a part of God's nature, nor is it something that God wants.

Theological systems that overemphasize God's omnipotence and God's predetermined plan for all eternity—and thus deemphasize the freedom that God gave created beings (human and supernatural)—have a particularly difficult time dealing with the problem of "good and evil." They all too easily portray God as the author and initiator, not only of good but also of evil, implying that it is ultimately God's fault that there is evil!

Theological systems that put a stronger emphasis on the free will that God gave created beings portray God somewhat differently. God does not control everything; rather, God is loving and faithful, even when we are confronted with evil and have become its victims. God respects the freedom given to supernatural beings and humanity. Evil's origin is not from God but from free creatures. The danger with this emphasis is that we might well wonder whether God's plans will ultimately succeed. If God is not in full control of all in the heavenlies and in the created universe, including the choices that people make, how can we be sure that God's purposes will be achieved?

My advice is not to let any theological system force our thinking into its mold, and especially not to subject texts to what our systems need them to say. Better to let Scripture speak for itself, even when we are unable to completely harmonize all its claims and work everything out in a logically coherent way.

According to Genesis, it all started when the first human pair allowed themselves to fall into temptation, when they ate the forbidden fruit. At that point they exercised their God-given freedom to turn away from God's good plan. When we keep reading, we realize that this was just the start. Soon we read of murder and of revenge (Genesis 4:8, 14, 24). Not long after, we learn that evil had gained the upper hand, so God decided to destroy a good deal of creation and begin anew (6:13). We read about the great flood, and how God preserved Noah, his family, and only as many animals as could be fit into the giant ark (6:9–9:19).

## TEMPTATION AND ITS CONSEQUENCES

In the beginning the world was "good," indeed "very good" (Genesis 1:10, 31). With the fall of the first human pair, a great deal was destroyed. God's image in humanity was not removed, but it became distorted. Tension and conflict arose between husband and wife, between garden and gardener, within human societies, and most seriously, between humans and their God. It got worse and worse until God responded in judgment and salvation. God sent the flood and, in many ways, started over. But even then, it took almost no time for evil to creep in again.

We soon find humanity trying to reach the heavens, to take control of their own destiny. The story of Babel (Genesis 11) is the story of human pride and God's new strategy both for fulfilling the first mandate ("fill the earth") and for controlling evil, scattering humanity in separate people groups all over the earth.

How do we read these first eleven chapters of Genesis? Many interpreters are convinced that the historicity of this section of the Bible is the most important thing we can defend. It really happened, and in precisely the way it is reported here. For others these are stories that tell us truth . . . not in a strictly *historical* sense, but the way things *are*! These are stories with true meanings.

Do we have to decide between *history* and *meaning*, as though it's one or the other? We may never know exactly how it all happened, but surely something serious must have happened to make God's original, completely good creation the way we experience it now. Something in history happened to block the full shalom that God intended. And if God holds humans accountable for the way things are, then regardless of any other influences, humans were not only victims; they were also rebels.

Genesis 3 truly helps us understand what "really happened." Yet grasping the meaning of the story should occupy our attention more than merely defending its historical accuracy. It is a story with the power to explain what is wrong with the world. It provides insight into why we also find ourselves turning away from God's good intentions and goals.

Throughout Scripture we see that the tempter is never far away, and sometimes temptation comes in ways remarkably like what happened in the garden. In Genesis 3:6, Eve recognized that the fruit was

1.  good for food;
2.  pleasing to the eye; and
3.  desirable for gaining wisdom.

Later texts reveal that Israel faced exactly these kinds of temptations, and often did not withstand them (see 1 Corinthians 10:7–10). And much later, when the church is warned against the "things of the world" in 1 John 2:16, these are described as

1.  the lust of the flesh;

2.  the lust of their eyes; and
3.  the pride of life.

It is not hard to see that this is similar to what Eve faced. Even the temptations that Jesus faced in the wilderness sound similar. Matthew 4:1–11 reports that he was tempted

1.  to turn stones into bread;
2.  to create a spectacle while testing God's faithfulness; and
3.  to compromise and thus gain worldly kingdoms.

Jesus was indeed tempted in all the ways we are (Hebrews 4:15). Whatever the nature of the historical event recorded in humanity's fall (Genesis 3), our primary concern should be to learn what the text teaches about God and this world:

- God created a good world, but the world did not remain good. Though much good remains, a great deal is now evil and destructive, and a great deal blocks the flow of God's goodness into the world.
- We were commissioned to be stewards, coworkers with God, joint participants in the course of history. These texts reveal why this is so important, and why it is so difficult. It is necessary because not all that happens in the universe corresponds to the unfolding of God's plan. It is difficult because we ourselves often live contrary to God's plan.
- The temptation to ignore and then rebel against God's revealed will did not come from within people; it came from outside humanity. In Genesis 3 we read about a snake. In other texts we read of a dragon, of the devil, of Satan, of the accuser (see Revelation 12:8–10). Humans are not only influenced by their own thoughts and plans.

God seeks to influence our thoughts and decisions. But so also does God's supernatural enemy.

- Sin has serious consequences. Even so, human rebellion and sin do not block God's purposes from being fulfilled. God remains faithful and builds bridges that create opportunities for us to find our way back into fellowship with God. God never ceases to invite us, to draw us back onto the path God has chosen for us.

## TWO KEY QUESTIONS

The first two chapters of the Bible describe a condition of paradise. Relationships are as they should be, all the way around—among people, between people and God, between people and God's creation. The chapters after that display how all these relationships begin to fall apart.

In Genesis 3:9, God asks Adam the first crucial question: "Where are you?" And in the next chapter, God asks Cain the second crucial question: "Where is your brother?" (4:9). As the larger biblical story unfolds, these two questions repeatedly take center stage. How is our relationship with God, and how can it be restored? How are our relationships with those around us, and how can strained and broken relationships be mended? The Ten Commandments are centered around these two key questions (Exodus 20:1–17). And so are the two commandments that Jesus called the greatest of them all: Love God and love your neighbor (Mark 12:29–31).

## THE WAY BACK

So far, we have bypassed one important but often misunderstood aspect of Genesis 3. I am referring to verses 14–15, which we will examine in the context of the whole Bible.

So the LORD God said to the serpent, "Because you have done this,

> "Cursed are you above all livestock
> and all wild animals!
> You will crawl on your belly
> and you will eat dust
> all the days of your life.
> And I will put enmity
> between you and the woman,
> and between your offspring and hers;
> he will crush your head,
> and you will strike his heel."

Theologians call this text the protevangelium, the "first gospel," the first announcement of good news, the first indication that God will provide a way back into fellowship with the Creator. God is not finished with this rebellious human family. They will still have offspring, and the conflict between God and the serpent will continue, with humanity caught in the middle. One day there will be an ultimate showdown. The snake will make its desperate attack and will strike at the heel of the woman's offspring. But the snake will not be the final victor. Its head will be crushed by the heel of the woman's offspring. In the end, the great enemy of God and humanity will be defeated. We will end up on the winner's side. Now that really is good news!

This text raises significant questions. Where, when, and how will this last battle take place? What happens after that? And perhaps most important: Who is (or are) the offspring of the woman who will gain that final victory?

We begin our observations with the final question. The Sunday school answer comes easily: *Jesus* will defeat the enemy.

Jesus is the victor! Jesus tramples Satan under his heel. Indeed, "offspring of the woman" might even be the first hint that Jesus will be born of a virgin. If this is our answer, perhaps a surprise awaits us as we examine the Scriptures more closely.

## "UNDER THE FEET"

We already encountered the image of being "under the feet" in the preceding chapter of this book. "You made them rulers over the works of your hands; you put everything under their feet" (Psalm 8:6). It is an almost universal image. I have in my files a newspaper article originating with the Associated Press that provides a captivating picture. The picture was taken on May 20, 1997, as rebels took captive a group of government troops in Kinshasa, capital of Congo (today the Democratic Republic of the Congo). The title visible below the picture is "Victor and Vanquished." The rebel's heel is firmly planted on the head of the captive soldier. There is no attempt here to injure. If that were the rebel's goal, the gun in his hand would be a far more effective instrument. Instead, the whole picture screams, "Look who is the victor here!" In other words, "heel on the head" means "conqueror"!

Why don't we sense any of this violent conquest when we read Psalm 8:6: "You put everything under their feet"? Because the expression "under their feet" is used in two related yet very different ways within the Bible.

*Psalm 8 is a picture of peace—of shalom!* It illustrates the role that humanity has been given, designed for the ultimate flourishing of humanity and all creation (see Genesis 1:28). It is a picture of what "subdue and rule over" is *supposed* to be all about (see Psalm 72). Everything is in right relationship with everything else. God is on top (God is a ten!); humanity is commissioned, as God's representatives, to "rule" so that there can be shalom; weaker elements of creation are thus cared for, whereas stronger elements are prevented from misusing their power.

*Genesis 3:15 is a picture of conflict—of shalom destroyed!* The snake does not willingly take up its proper position under the heel of the woman's offspring. On the contrary, the snake is there because it loses in a desperate but failed attempt to become the conqueror. Unfortunately, far too many situations resemble the photograph from Kinshasa. People fight each other with fists, machine guns, or more powerful weapons still. Or they rule over each other with terror, with misused power, with abusive relationships. Yes, indeed, the picture language of "under the feet" is universal.

## TRAMPLING THE ENEMY

We need to consider carefully what the Bible does with this picture. Perhaps the Sunday school answer is not the whole story. We begin with Romans 16:19–20, the New Testament (NT) text that most nearly reflects the wording of Genesis 3:15. Paul is writing to believers in Rome and praising them because, through their obedience to God, they are making good progress in the battle between good and evil.

Then comes the wonderful promise: "The God of peace will soon crush Satan under your feet" (Romans 16:20). Under whose feet? Jesus' feet? No, under the feet of the believers. Yes, it is God's victory, for God is the one who crushes Satan. But the feet are ours. The God of peace (*eirēnē* in Greek, but behind it the Hebrew word *shalom*) uses us to defeat Satan under *our feet*.

And this pattern (God wins the battle through us) is pervasive in the New Testament. In various texts we read about Jesus sending out his disciples on a mission. In pursuit of their mission, they announce God's victory. But in doing so, they regularly combat evil powers, casting out demons and facing evil opposition. As they return, they report with great joy, "Lord, even the demons submit to us in your name" (Luke 10:17). Jesus assures them that in this he sees evidence of the casting down of Satan. "I saw Satan fall like lightning from heaven" (10:18). Then Jesus explains why all this was possible: "I have given you authority to trample on snakes and scorpions and to overcome all the power of the enemy; nothing will harm you" (10:19). Jesus had given them power to trample on snakes! Jesus had passed on his authority to them. They were his representatives and had indeed emerged victorious over "snakes." They had been involved in crushing Satan under their feet.

## VICTORY DAY

Perhaps the most impressive picture of all is the one drawn in Revelation 12. Starting at verse 7, we read of the defeat of God's great enemy:

> Michael and his angels fought against the dragon, and the dragon and his angels fought back. But he was not strong enough, and they lost their place in heaven. The great dragon was hurled down—that ancient snake called the devil, or Satan, who leads the whole world astray. He was hurled to the earth, and his angels with him. (12:7–9)

In John's vision of this great battle, a heavenly voice is then heard to exclaim:

> Now have come the salvation and the power
> and the kingdom of our God,
> and the authority of his Messiah.

For the accuser of our brothers and sisters,
    who accuses them before our God day and night,
    has been hurled down.
(Revelation 12:10)

But who won this great victory? If we read no more, the answers would seem obvious. God is the victor, God together with his Messiah. Michael, the archangel, and his fellow angels are involved as well. This is an entirely heavenly battle! But the writer of Revelation says something else.

"They [our brothers and sisters] triumphed over him" (12:11a). The battle is won in the heavenly realms; but the battle is won by "our brothers and sisters." Precisely those being accused by the devil become agents of God's victory. And how do they accomplish that? Here is the crucial point of the text: "They triumphed over him by the blood of the Lamb and by the word of their testimony; they did not love their lives so much as to shrink from death" (12:11).

The Lamb's blood made the victory possible—not the Lamb's sword, but the Lamb's blood. The victory did not come because the Lamb took the life of the enemy. The victory came because the Lamb gave up his own life for the enemy. *They* win through his blood. "Our brothers and sisters" are the faithful believers ready to give up their own lives as well. They are followers of Jesus, right through to their own death. They have learned from him that the true and final victory over evil is not accomplished through the sword and the shedding of blood. The true and final victory is gained through sacrificing their own lives in faithfulness to the Lamb who did that first.

The great cry of celebration at the beginning of this text is repeated at the end. "Therefore rejoice, you heavens and you who dwell in them! But woe to the earth and the sea, because the devil has gone down to you! He is filled with fury, because he knows that his time is short" (12:12).

So something else becomes clear. This is not a victory that takes place only at the end of world history. The victory has already been achieved, but the battle on earth still rages. We are assured that God is the final victor, yet the texts have also elucidated: The victory in the heavenly realms is not won by God alone, not even by God through the death and resurrection of Jesus alone. *They* defeated the enemy—*they*, the followers of the Lamb. They (we!) will participate in the blessings of victory, but only after they (we!) have participated in the battle. But the texts also underscore that they did not win the battle alone. They won *through the blood of the Lamb* (12:11).

We, the followers of Jesus, a renewed humanity through the New Adam, regain what was lost when the first Adam sinned. We together with our God are the shapers of history, we are comrades in God's army, in a battle still raging to achieve complete victory over evil. We join God in bridging the gap between the present reality and the fulfillment of that great shalom project that has always been God's goal. We participate in trampling on snakes—in neutralizing the destructive devices of God's great enemy.

## PARTNERS IN THE VICTORY

Ephesians 1 is another significant text for this theme. Paul is sharing with his readers the content of his prayers for them (Ephesians 1:17–19). He prays that they might have the Spirit of wisdom and revelation so that with enlightened eyes they might recognize important invisible realities. These include the fact that they have a great future hope, that God's mighty power has been made available to believers, and that all this results in a great inheritance not yet fully experienced. Paul sees the various components fitting together like this:

- It may seem hard to believe, but we really are awaiting a great future hope.
- We will not catch glimpses of this, nor even believe it possible, unless we are given enlightened eyes.
- This hope will become a full reality when God finally invests all of God's great power to bring it about.
- But God has already shown us in history how great that power is.
- That demonstration happened when God raised Jesus from death.

Jesus' resurrection provides the lynchpin for the whole final victory of God. It is the evidence within history that God's power is sufficient to gain the final victory in the end.

The resurrection of Jesus also verifies something else. It proves that the battle strategies Jesus used are the ones that will finally get the job done. Jesus did not come to annihilate enemies; Jesus came as a peacemaker, came with the most powerful weapons of all: nonviolence and self-sacrifice. And Jesus did all that because he was confident that God's power was sufficient even to turn back the power of death.

In *The Lion, the Witch, and the Wardrobe,* C. S. Lewis explains the deepest magic of the universe: "When a willing victim who had committed no treachery was killed in a traitor's stead, the Table would crack and Death itself would start working backward."[1]

Paul writes eloquently and movingly about the resurrection of Jesus and what that great event accomplished. In the process, he again contributes to the theme we are exploring: how and when God's enemy is finally defeated, when and how its "head is struck" (to use the language of Genesis 3:15), and by whom God's enemy is finally trampled underfoot.

Paul speaks of God's power, which "he exerted when he raised Christ from the dead and seated him at his right hand in the heavenly realms, far above all rule and authority, power and dominion, and every name that is invoked, not only in the present age but also in the one to come. And God placed all things *under his feet* and appointed him to be head over everything" (Ephesians 1:20–22, emphasis added).

In the end, the Sunday school answer is proved true after all! God put everything under *Jesus'* feet, and "everything" includes all God's enemies. God wins the victory through Jesus, and through Jesus alone . . . so it appears up to this point.

But then we are surprised once more. "God placed all things under his feet and appointed him to be head over everything for the church, which is his body, the fullness of him who fills everything in every way" (Ephesians 1:22–23). Everything will be conquered by Jesus; everything will be under Jesus' feet—except for us. We, the church, will *not* be under Christ's feet. On the contrary, *we will be Christ's feet!* Jesus is only the Head. Jesus and his church together will gain the final victory. Under *Christ's* feet turns out to mean under *our* feet, for we are the body of Christ.

The protevangelium of Genesis 3:15 is fulfilled in Jesus and in all those united to Jesus as part of his body. Precisely because the victory belongs to Jesus, it also belongs to us. Jesus not only gained the victory on our behalf, but also wins the victory with our participation. Head and body stand up at the end as the final victors. The battle is not won with swords or any other form of violence. It is won through a willingness to sacrifice ourselves in faithfulness and in hope, and then through the release of God's power, resurrection power that conquers death and those who deal in it.

## WHY IS IT IMPORTANT TO PAY ATTENTION TO GENESIS 3–11?

Without these Genesis chapters, we would know far too little about why the world is as it is, how God will fulfill God's creation purposes despite the presence of evil, and what role is given to us. We are those who have received God's matchless grace. We have been recruited to join God's side in the great battle that rages through history in this time between the times.

## *Questions for discussion*

---

1.  Do you understand the temptation of Adam and Eve primarily as a one-time event in the garden, or as a portrait of the way all of us are tempted to be drawn away from God's good plans for us?

2.  "Where are you?" "Where is your brother?" Where do you see these two great questions dealt with in Scripture in ways that help us understand our two greatest responsibilities?

3.  "Precisely because the victory belongs to Jesus, it also belongs to us. Jesus not only gained the victory on our behalf, but also wins the victory with our participation. Head and body stand up at the end as the final victors. The battle is not won with swords or any other form of violence. It is won through a willingness to sacrifice ourselves in faithfulness and in hope, and then through the release of God's power, resurrection power that conquers death and those who deal in it." How do you respond to these claims?

# GOD, THE ONE WHO BLESSES

## *(Genesis 12–36)*

*I was sent only to the lost sheep of Israel. —Matthew 15:24*

*Many will come from the east and the west, and will take their places at the feast with Abraham, Isaac and Jacob in the kingdom of heaven. —Matthew 8:11*

These paradoxical statements represent well God's strategy for the salvation of the world. Many world religions claim that salvation is achieved by adopting the right belief system, living a morally acceptable life, or practicing prescribed religious exercises. Scripture maintains that salvation is not at all a human achievement. It is a divine achievement. God designs a strategy and over millennia works in history to achieve it, ultimately accomplishing it through Jesus.

To be sure, *accessing* the salvation that God offers involves human responses, choices, and participation. But God is always the initiator, and God always recruits those who have experienced God's salvation to be conduits through which others may experience it as well.

A major theme of the Old Testament is that God calls and prepares a special people group, Israel, so that through them the good news of God's saving grace may reach the ends of the earth. It is a very long-range strategy, as we shall see, and one that Jesus fully embraced and embodied in his ministry. Jesus concentrated his mission on Israel. Why? Because his goal was the salvation of the whole world.

❖

A massive turning point in world history begins with the story of Abraham. In many ways it is a new story, a story about one man called by God, one couple chosen for a specific mission, a very slowly growing family, and in the end a Semitic people group, one among many in the Middle East. It is a story set in one small corner of the globe. Why does God concentrate on the individual person, the individual family, the individual people group? God does it because God's concern is always for the whole world. This paradox deserves our careful attention.

## GOD CARES ABOUT THE WHOLE WORLD

God is *always* concerned about the whole world. The creation narratives in Genesis 1 and 2 already reveal this. And after the fall, it is the whole world that God desires to save, renew, and lead to its ultimate destiny in God's plan. That is revealed in many places: in the protevangelium (Genesis 3:15); in the story of the expansion of human society (Genesis 4–5); in the narrative of God's judgment and salvation through the great flood (Genesis 6–8); in the account of God's new covenant with Noah and his descendants (so therefore with all of humanity; Genesis 9); in the Table of Nations (Genesis 10). Even the story of the Tower of Babel (Genesis 11) reveals how all the nations of the earth repeated the sins of Adam and Eve (grasping for divinity), and how they were therefore scattered from God's presence and thus need God's salvation and restoration. The first eleven chapters of the Bible are all written with a focus on the whole world and all its peoples.

In Genesis 12, God begins to concentrate on the individual. It will be God's strategy to fulfill the unchanging purpose of winning back the entire world.

God decided to create a brand-new people group. This people group would become a model to the others, demonstrating what it means to live in relationship with God, to be faithful stewards of God's creation. So God begins with an individual, and thus with one family. Out of this one family, God will create a new people group. God will specially commission them for a distinct mission. They will show the world what it means to belong to God, to be saved by God, and to become channels through whom others will find salvation. The goal is to win back the whole world, to recover what the enemy had taken away.

Note that God did not choose an existing nation for this mission; God created a brand-new nation. We know what normally characterizes people groups. They come into being when historical and geographical circumstances as well as familial relationships and shared experiences gradually produce unique dialects, unique forms of artistic expression, unique clothing styles, unique traditions, and a host of other distinctive characteristics. Observers can recognize to which "people group" individuals belong, and in particular, "insiders" can very easily detect differences when "outsiders" are among them. God decided that no people group, *as a normal people group*, would be able to fulfill the crucial mandate God had in mind. God's new strategy required a special sort of people group, for only in this way could the whole world be won.

And so God chose to create an entirely new, and new *kind of*, people group. This would be a people group not defined by the normal marks of ethnicity and nationhood. It would be the result of God's personal intervention in history. Indeed, God would repeatedly intervene. The birth of this new people group would be unusual enough to signal that God was changing what we know as the normal course of human history.

God began with a man named Abram, later renamed Abraham. He would become the father of a whole new people group, "the people of Israel." But this people group would be more than that; it would be "the people of God." Israel would become God's means of saving all the nations and would be qualified for that role precisely by being *unlike* all the other nations. As we will see, every time this people group aimed to be "like all the other nations" (1 Samuel 8:20), they became less and less able to fulfill their primary mandate. Only a people group unlike the others could be used by God to lead the others back to God.

## GOD WRITES A NEW CHAPTER

On the day when God called Abram, virtually everything continued its normal course. For the rest of the world, life simply went on as usual. Seasons came and went, products were brought to market to be bought and sold, wars were fought, weddings celebrated, births and deaths commemorated. But in one tiny corner of the earth, God had begun to write a new chapter in the history of the world.

The LORD had said to Abram, "Go from your country, your people and your father's household to the land I will show you.

"I will make you into a great nation,
    and I will bless you;
I will make your name great,
    and you will be a blessing.
I will bless those who bless you,
    and whoever curses you I will curse;
and all peoples on earth
    will be blessed through you."

So Abram went, as the LORD had told him. (Genesis 12:1–4a)

One day Abram lived among all his relatives in the city of Harran. The next day he was preparing for a journey, a journey into the unknown—that is, unknown to Abram, but not to God. God had a plan and purpose in mind, something brand new in world history.

"*Go from your country.*" God would be creating a people group whose existence would not depend on having a country, possessions, or a homeland of their own. Thousands of years later an anonymous preacher would summarize the call of Abraham:

By faith Abraham, when called to go to a place he would later receive as his inheritance, obeyed and went, even though he did not know where he was going. By faith he made his home in the promised land like a stranger in a foreign country; he lived in tents, as did Isaac and Jacob, who were heirs with him of the same promise. For he was looking forward to the city with foundations, whose architect and builder is God. (Hebrews 11:8–10)

God had a special place for this new people group, but that place would not be defined by geography.

*"Go from your people and your father's household."* The people group that God was about to create would descend from previous parents and grandparents, as do all the peoples of the earth. But in significant ways it would be unlike all the rest. The defining parent of this new people group would not be Abram's father, Terah, but Abram's Father, God! In this utterly new and unusual people group, the primary relationships would not be blood relationships but covenant relationships. Complete strangers would become siblings in God's new family. Thousands of years later, Jesus addressed this very issue when he asked, "'Who are my mother and my brothers?' Then he looked at those seated in a circle around him and said, 'Here are my mother and my brothers! Whoever does God's will is my brother and sister and mother'" (Mark 3:33–35).

*"Go to the land I will show you."* God did not want Abram to see the whole picture right up front, to be given enough information that he could evaluate his options and make a calculated decision whether he would agree to the terms and conditions of God's proposal. Abram was called to trust God. God wanted Abram to give an unconditional yes, to take faithful steps of obedience even in those situations where Abram had no idea where God was leading him.

*"I will make you into a great nation."* At first things did not look very promising at all. Abram was already seventy-five, and his wife Sarai (later called Sarah) was not much younger. They were childless, and yet were promised that they would be the parents and grandparents of a great nation. How was that supposed to happen?

*"I will make you into a great nation, and I will bless you; I will make your name great, and you will be a blessing. I*

*will bless those who bless you, and whoever curses you I will curse; and all peoples on earth will be blessed through you."* God had already pronounced a blessing on the first human pair, Adam and Eve. Along with the blessing God gave them a great assignment. Now God pronounced a blessing on a new couple, one that would be instrumental in God's great project of leading all humanity back to God. And as before, with the blessing, comes the assignment. God always takes the initiative, pronounces blessings, gifts us with grace, showers us with love. God never does that merely for our personal benefit and pleasure. We are blessed to be a blessing to others.

Right from the start, God made it clear to Abram. This is not about you: this is about all the others. This is not about the people group that you will be used to bring into being. This is about all the other people groups who will find their way back to God through them. God wants to create a new people of God to be a light on the hill, shining in order that others might find their way, their way through life and their way back to God. Much later, God would say to some of Abraham's descendants, a faithful minority within Israel: "It is too small a thing for you to be my servant to restore the tribes of Jacob and bring back those of Israel I have kept. I will also make you a light for the Gentiles, that my salvation may reach to the ends of the earth" (Isaiah 49:6).

Later still, Jesus said to those who declared themselves willing to take up God's commission to Israel: "You are the light of the world. . . . Let your light shine before others, that they may see your good deeds and glorify your Father in heaven" (Matthew 5:14–16).

*"So Abram went, as the Lord had told him."* God had called someone for the very special purpose of starting something brand new. Abram proved willing to take the required steps of

faith and obedience. I can imagine his relatives' astonishment. Perhaps his whole city tried to argue sense into him. "Have you gone stark raving mad? Some god wants to lead you away from here? Don't be ridiculous!" I imagine Abram's move out of Harran caused quite a stir. But I also imagine that nobody knew, not even Abram, that God had begun to set in motion a brand-new strategy for the salvation of the whole world.

## GOD MAKES AND KEEPS A PROMISE

It would be a mistake to assume that from Genesis 12 onward, God's participation in the world was limited to what God did with Abraham and his descendants. God remained the creator, sustainer, and Lord of the whole earth. God's glory continued to be reflected in the beauties of nature. God continued, and continues even to this day, to guarantee the rhythms of day and night, summer and winter, seedtime and harvest, generations coming and going. All humans everywhere continue to bear the image of God. The human conscience continues to bear witness that this is a moral universe and that the Creator holds us accountable. Yet the call of Abram also instituted something new. From then on God would be about the business of showing the world that God's presence is most evident among those who, like Abram, are prepared to respond to God's call with faith and obedience.

The story of Abram has many turning points, many ups and downs. Names are changed (Abram to Abraham, Sarai to Sarah). People move here and there (Abraham and Sarah even live for a while in Egypt). There are tensions in the family. Poorly devised human strategies for expediting God's promise backfire. The resulting tensions, for example between Sarah and Hagar, and then between their children, Isaac and Ishmael, prove to have repercussions for generations, some affecting the world even today. Much that is done falls far short of God's perfect plan.

Yet God has promised! God declares that out of Abraham a great nation will emerge. And God keeps the promise. God keeps it in faithfulness to God's own covenant, even though humans so often fail to keep faith with God. Theologian Bernhard Ott describes it like this:

> People live in the tension between promise and fulfillment. Those who know the Abraham story know full well that God's promises are sometimes fulfilled only much later and after many hindrances have been overcome. . . . God's project . . . contained the promise that Abraham's family would become a great nation. And yet Abraham and Sarah were growing old and this promise was not being fulfilled. They waited and waited, and, before their lives ended, that great nation consisted of exactly one son. They lived in this tension. . . . We all live in the same tension.[1]

After God finally keeps the promise of a son, God requires of Abraham another step of faith, another unconditional yes. God sends Abraham on another journey without specifying the destination. This time, however, it is not his wife Sarah who accompanies Abraham, but their son Isaac. God instructs Abraham to prepare to offer to God his dearly loved son Isaac, just as if Isaac were a sacrificial lamb. Abraham is to build an altar, bind up Isaac upon it, dedicate the offering, and then sacrifice Isaac to God.

Child sacrifice was not unknown in Abraham's pagan religious environment (see Deuteronomy 12:31). But was Abraham's God now requiring such sacrifice? Was Abraham to sacrifice the child of promise? The whole idea made absolutely no sense. Yet Abraham trusted God and began to prepare.

Centuries later the writer to the Hebrews interpreted Abraham's willingness to obey the voice of God as follows:

> By faith Abraham, when God tested him, offered Isaac as a sacrifice. He who had embraced the promises was about to sacrifice his one and only son, even though God had said to him, "It is through Isaac that your offspring will be reckoned." Abraham reasoned that God could even raise the dead, and so in a manner of speaking he did receive Isaac back from death. (Hebrews 11:17–19 NIV)

Abraham was willing to say yes unconditionally and to follow through to the end. At the last possible moment, God stopped Abraham and supplied a substitute sacrifice, a ram caught in the bushes. Thus, we are taught what saving grace is all about: God supplying the sacrifice necessary to provide for our salvation. We owe God all that we are and have, including the very breath of life, for God is our creator and Lord. If God were to demand the very life of the creature, God would have every right to take it. But Scripture teaches us that God accepts and provides a substitute for the life God has a right to take. That theme is developed all the way through the Scriptures. All who sin (that includes all of us) owe God our very lives. But God will accept a substitute.

Abraham's story is followed by Isaac's story, then Jacob's, then Joseph's. Gradually, a new people group comes into being. Along the way we have examples of unusual births, as if God wanted to say, These are "children born not of natural descent, nor of human decision or a husband's will, but born of God" (John 1:13).

Isaac, the child of promise, is born after his parents are far too old to have children. In Isaac's family, against all cultural expectations, secondborn Jacob, not firstborn Esau, is commissioned to carry on the family promise and obligation. Jacob's family, perhaps taking a nod from Jacob himself, includes an inordinate amount of conflict between the wives and concubines. That discord then carries on among their children, and yet God plans to form out of *all* the sons of Jacob a new people group.

Only a sequence of miracles could have resulted in the formation of the people of Israel. God wants to make unmistakably clear that this new people group will not be formed or held together by the normal processes of nature and human sociology. This will be a people group that transcends all natural family bonds. Membership in it will not be by natural means, but by a mutual covenant with the one true God, who will make of them a holy people. Without that, and without God's repeated interventions, this people group will never hold together or survive. But with that, it will be used by God for the salvation of the whole world.

## GOD ELECTS A PEOPLE GROUP

Why did God choose just one people group and not, right from the start, all of them? At this point we are confronted with the biblical theme of election. The topic is theologically challenging, but we often make it more complicated than it needs to be.

Two points should be kept front and center. First, election in Scripture is rarely applied to an *individual person*. Election normally applies to a *people group*. Through a series of miraculous interventions, God brings a special people group of God's own choosing into existence. When individual people are called, it is not for their own election, but to bring into existence (or in some cases to rescue, restore, or lead) God's people group. The election of individuals is always for the sake of the larger people group. In fact, individuals are rarely, if ever, *forced* into the roles into which they are recruited. They may be called, invited, or challenged, but their response is still needed. It is their choice to fulfill the role for which they were "elected," or to resist the call of God. Only rarely does God seem to put inordinate pressure on those whom God calls. God gives every human a free will, and the norm is that God respects the choices each of us makes, even when those choices are to reject God's call. Election is not God overriding human choice; election is God setting aside for a special mission a people group, and then inviting individuals to live in covenant faithfulness to, and perform concrete roles within, this elect people of God.

We often underestimate how fluid the boundaries of the OT people of God actually were. People could, by their own choices, cross the boundaries, both going out and coming in. It is not as though one specific ethnic group was "the chosen people" and all others were the "unchosen." Those within ethnic and national Israel who were unfaithful and disobedient might well "be cut off from Israel" (Exodus 12:15). And those formerly of other ethnicities and other nations could, simply by choosing to do so, become members of the people of God. That is what the Moabite Ruth did when she declared, "Your people will be my people and your God my God" (Ruth 1:16). The point is this: God normally elects a people group and not an individual, and those who choose to become and to remain members of the group are "the elect." Far from being the alternative to human choice, election depends on it.

A second important point: *Election brings significant responsibility.* God always elects as part of a larger project. God elects one people group because it is God's plan, through one people group, to bless all the other peoples.

A text that many have found troubling (understandably) is Romans 9:13. Paul quotes Malachi 1:2–3, a text that itself references Genesis 25:23. In the Romans text, God says: "Jacob I loved, but Esau I hated." Paul's point is that God chose the secondborn Jacob, rather than the firstborn Esau, to be the bearer of the promise, the one elected to carry on the legacy and the commission after Grandfather Abraham and Father Isaac. To our sensibilities, this seems completely unfair. How can a just and fair God select one person for special blessing and shove the other to the side—worse still, *hate* the other?

Paul addresses this problem in the passage where the troubling sentence is found ("Jacob I loved, but Esau I hated."). Paul's discussion continues: "What then shall we say? Is God unjust? Not at all! For he says to Moses, 'I will have mercy on whom I have mercy, and I will have compassion on whom I have compassion.' It does not, therefore, depend on human desire or effort, but on God's mercy" (Romans 9:14–16).

Some have taken this passage to mean something like "You think God is being unfair? Well, that is none of your business. If God wants to act unfairly, who are you to take offense? God can do exactly what God wants to do? It's God's prerogative! God's choices and decisions are not subject to our human scrutiny and evaluation."

But that is an attitude quite foreign to the Scriptures! Elsewhere in Scripture we read repeatedly that God's justice is evident to all. Indeed, the Scriptures emphasize the importance of God's justice being evident and recognized by all. Psalm 98:2, for example, declares: "He has shown the nations that he does what is right" (NIrV).

God is not unjust, as humans often are, or capricious, as pagan gods often appear to be (see Numbers 23:19). God loves without condition, pouring out gifts of grace on the evil and on the good (see Matthew 5:44–45). What then is Paul trying to communicate in Romans 9 with his reference to God "loving" one and "hating" the other?

Paul is using a figure of speech, one well known in his literary context. Figures of speech can be notoriously difficult to translate. Word-for-word translations often miss the mark by miles. For example, the English expression "His idea was way out in left field" sounds extremely strange in German: "Seine Idee war weit draußen im linken Feld." Or perhaps we should turn it around. The German expression "Er fuhr mit einem Affenzahn" sounds pretty ridiculous in English: "He drove with a monkey's tooth." Figures of speech are *not* to be taken literally!

In English, the word *hate* has a specific meaning: It means hate!—social rejection, feelings of animosity, ill-will toward another. But in Scripture, the word for "hate" has other meanings. In contrast with the verb "to love" (*agapaō*), it signals priorities. "Love" means giving first priority, whereas "to hate" (*miseō*) means *not* giving first priority. That seems obvious in Luke 14:26, where Jesus says, "If anyone comes to me and does not hate father and mother, wife and children, brothers and sisters—yes, even their own life—such a person cannot be my disciple."

Jesus is not commanding us to literally hate our families; just as obviously, God does not literally hate Esau. Some modern translations choose to word it like this: "You cannot be my disciple, unless you love me more than you love your father and mother" (Luke 14:26 CEV). *The Message* paraphrase proposes that "hate" should be understood as "let go of." Jesus is not talking about literal love and hate. Jesus is talking about priorities. In cases of irreconcilable conflict, where will our priorities lie? In the end, who will be given first priority, and who will be given second priority?

Other texts make the same point, sometimes with similar wording, sometimes with other expressions. Matthew 6:24, for example, says this: "No one can serve two masters. Either you will hate the one and love the other, or you will be devoted to the one and despise the other." We know that people can serve two masters, but only as long as the demands of each are fully compatible. When two masters make mutually exclusive claims on our lives, a choice must be made: Whom will I ultimately serve? If my employer makes a demand on me that my Lord forbids me to carry out, then my response reveals who my true "Lord" is. I must decide which Lord I will "love" and which I will "hate"—except that is not a clearly understood expression in English, so nobody would word it like that. We would more likely say it the way Peter words it, "We must obey God rather than human beings!" (Acts 5:29).

Jacob was elected to play the leading role; Esau was selected to be in the second position. "But that is still unfair!" we may be inclined to protest. Well, not necessarily. God was not literally hating Esau, or even setting Esau aside. On the contrary, God was choosing Jacob to be a blessing to Esau. Jacob was to inherit the promise and the responsibility first given to Abraham: "All peoples on earth will be blessed though you" (Genesis 12:3). So why then should it still seem unfair?

Perhaps an example helps. If I could succeed in always making sure my wife was the very most important person in my life, always and in every way, I think she would have it pretty good. (I hope so, at least!) But what if I succeeded in always making her the *second* most important person in life, consistently second in my heart and in my priorities *to Jesus only*? Would she then be disadvantaged? I doubt it. I suspect she would have it even better! I am convinced that when we succeed in giving Jesus the first place in our heart, the first priority in all our choices, those closest to us benefit from our priorities. If we love God with all our heart, soul, mind, and strength, then this will always advantage, not disadvantage, the people whom we also love.

So it is when God elects one party for special honor and responsibility (like Jacob). The intended outcome is that blessings will flow to all the others (like Esau). When God's elect people group enjoys its covenant privileges and lives out its covenant responsibilities, this will always advantage, and not disadvantage, all the others. Then the story of Abraham and his descendants reaches its goal.

## GOD'S NEW PROJECT HAS BEGUN

We have looked at a few key texts and themes from a very long section of Scripture (Genesis 12–36). It is a rather detailed story of the first three generations of God's chosen strategy for redeeming and blessing the whole world. God had promised Abraham, "I will surely bless you and make your descendants as numerous as the stars in the sky and as the sand on the seashore" (22:17).

By the end of the book of Genesis, this people group consisted of about seventy people, no more. There's Jacob, his children, his grandchildren. That's it. Yes, they are all related—they are one family. But God is emphasizing: This is not about blood relationships; this is not about common customs and traditions, not about culture and language, not about geographical and historical backgrounds. This is about a covenant that God is making with those called into a special mission. This is about a promise made to those who respond to God's offer and demand; this is about a people of God unlike the normal "peoples of the earth." Had God wanted to work with an ordinary people group, there would been many to choose. Instead, God created a brand-new people group—or better said, God is still about the business of creating a brand-new people group, a community of faith that lives differently from all the peoples of the earth so that God can use it to bless and save them.

## WHY IS IT IMPORTANT TO READ THE NARRATIVES IN GENESIS 12–36?

How are these old stories about the creation of ancient Israel still relevant for the NT church? Very simple: These stories are our own historical roots. We are the children of Abraham. The New Testament calls us "the Israel of God" (Galatians 6:16). The most important terms and descriptors applying to Israel in the Old Testament are applied to the church in the New Testament. (This does *not* mean that the NT church replaced Israel as God's chosen people. We will return to this important issue in chapter 6.) We read Genesis 12–36 to know how our *own story* began, the story of God's chosen people, elected to be a blessing for the whole world.

# *Questions for discussion*

1. "God's concern is always for the whole world." How is this evident in the first thirty-six chapters of the Bible (and the first three chapters of this book)? How do we see that God always has the whole world in mind when God deals with the individual?

2. Consider how the Abraham narrative demonstrates the following claims: "God wants to make unmistakably clear that this new people group will not be formed or held together by the normal processes of nature and human sociology. This will be a people group that transcends all natural family bonds. Membership in it will not be by natural means, but by a mutual covenant with the one true God, who will make of them a holy people."

3. "When God's elect people group enjoys its covenant privileges and lives out its covenant responsibilities, this will always be to the advantage, and not the disadvantage, of all the others." How is this explanation of the concept of "election" confirmed in the Scriptures? How is it confirmed in your experience?

# GOD, THE GREAT DELIVERER

## *(Genesis 37–Exodus 15)*

*Father, forgive them, for they do not know what they are doing. —Luke 23:34*

*He has sent me . . . to set the oppressed free. —Luke 4:18*

Joseph and Moses are two OT leaders who, at different times, play prominent roles in ancient Egypt and are used by God to deliver Israel. And both of them prefigure Jesus in significant ways. Just like Joseph in ancient times, Jesus suffered at the hands of his own people, yet saved them in the end. Instead of wreaking vengeance on his enemies, he forgave them. Just like Moses in ancient times, Jesus was miraculously protected as a child, and lived to set the oppressed free and lead them.

In every way, Jesus superseded Joseph and Moses and all other OT servants of God. Indeed, Jesus was the fulfillment of everything they prepared for and foreshadowed. Yet OT leaders were so much more than "stages on the way to Jesus."

They were God's chosen servants to enact the purposes of God in their generation as each contributed to the formation and ultimately the deliverance of the people of God.

❖

The previous chapter mostly paid attention to Abraham, Isaac, and Jacob (the man whom God "elected" and then his son and grandson, those who inherited the call and the commission after him). These men, along with their wives and families, were chosen by God to represent a brand-new strategy for the salvation of the whole world. They answered God's call with a decisive yes, and thus took the risk of joining God's project, God's strategy designed to benefit not only this growing people group, but all the other peoples of the world as well.

This was a very long-range project. First, God would bring into existence a people group through the normal course of human population growth, and with a very slow beginning at that. This new people group would then learn to listen to God's voice and to follow God's leading. It would become a nation *unlike* all the other nations. Among God's people there would be no abuse of power, no unchecked accumulation of personal wealth, no false worship, no condoning of sinful behavior. At least that was the plan! All observers would recognize that this unique people group was a living demonstration of the good life, where all were taken care of, where each lived under God's blessing. God's people would not be the *real* owners of the land and property that God would give them. *God* would be the real owner; God's people would be stewards and caretakers on God's behalf.

Those observing Israel would be drawn to Israel's God. Israel would be blessed, but more importantly, through Israel all the nations of the world would be blessed. This was not merely about Israel's privilege. Israel had been set apart for a great mission. Remember, God's concern is always for the whole world. Jacob was elected and called, but this was to be to Esau's advantage. Israel was called, but this was to be to the advantage and not the disadvantage of the Egyptians, the Amorites, the Canaanites, and all the other peoples around them.

What a grand project! Yet when we reach the end of Genesis, not much of it has been accomplished. The people of Israel (and simultaneously the people of God) consisted of a mere seventy people. And they were not living in the promised land. They were economic refugees in Egypt. The last part of the book of Genesis tells us how this situation came about. To understand what happened, we begin with Joseph's dream (Genesis 37).

## A NOT-VERY-MODEL PEOPLE GROUP

Dreams usually do not emerge without something significant generating them. When a man dreams that his parents and siblings fall down and worship him, chances are something is going on in the family. This dreamer, Joseph, was heir to at least three generations of family conflict and competition. There were already significant conflicts between Joseph's great-grandmother Sarah and the enslaved Hagar, whom Joseph's great-grandfather Abraham had taken as a concubine (see Genesis 16:4–5), a conflict then transferred to their children, Grandpa Isaac and Great-Uncle Ishmael (21:9). And then there's the conflict between Joseph's grandmother Rebekah and his grandfather Isaac, each favoring one of their twin sons, and Rebekah helping one of them trick the other one out the family inheritance (see Genesis 27). And what consequences that had—disappointment, hatred, deception, fear, and endless conflict among their descendants!

Joseph grew up in a household rocked with conflict and jealousy. His father Jacob had married two sisters and then taken additional concubines into his household. One need only read the narrative recounting the births of Jacob's sons to four different mothers, and in particular the naming of the children, to quickly recognize that competition ruled this household (see 29:31–30:24). When Jacob's favorite wife finally had a son, it was soon evident to everyone: "Now Israel [= Jacob] loved Joseph more than any of his other sons, because he had been born to him in his old age; and he made an ornate robe for him" (37:3).

Is it any wonder that the teenage Joseph had something of a superiority complex? He openly reported to his family the dream about all of them worshiping him, revealing both his inflated ego and his lack of tact. His brothers hated him. Are we surprised?

God is about the business of creating a model people group. This people group is not a particularly good model of what God has in mind. They seem, at least at this point in their history, to be no better than the people groups who do not know the one true God. Thus, even at this beginning stage of God's grand new project, God makes one thing clear: To be the people of God is not a human achievement; it is not a reward for good behavior. It is pure undeserved grace. Perhaps we should say it even more starkly: If God can create a "people of God" out of Abraham and his descendants, then presumably God could do it with anybody! To be the people of God is from beginning to end a *gift*, not a *reward*.

God had promised to make out of Abraham's descendants a people. "I will surely bless you and make your descendants as numerous as the stars in the sky and as the sand on the seashore" (22:17). Though humans fail God, God's promises never fail.

## HUMAN PLANNING AND GOD'S PLAN—JOSEPH

Joseph's brothers, reacting both to Joseph's dream and to the preferential treatment their father gave him, sold the haughty young dreamer to Midianite merchants, who in turn sold him to Potiphar, a political official in Egypt (Genesis 37:27, 36). Not long afterward, as a victim of false accusations, Joseph landed in jail. In time the dreamer became an interpreter of dreams, and through a series of surprising circumstances, and by the grace of God, Joseph was set free, and eventually earned the good graces of the pharaoh, who promoted him. He became the second most powerful man in the nation, with one primary responsibility: to protect the nation from starvation in the face of a coming drought and famine. Genesis 37–41 narrates the whole suspense-filled story.

In the end, Joseph's dreams of personal greatness came true. Among those saved from the famine we find Joseph's own family, those brothers who attempted to get rid of him, and Jacob, his father, the cause of much of the conflict and tragedy. In the Joseph narrative we see visible evidence of the prophetic word in Isaiah 55:9: "As the heavens are higher than the earth, so are my ways higher than your ways and my thoughts than your thoughts."

As a rule, God, who gave humans free choice in the first place, allows even those choices to stand which set humans against God's own plans and purposes. Yet God's plans and purposes never fail. *Despite* our choices, even our rebellious choices, indeed sometimes even *through* those choices, God fulfills divine plans and purposes. We see that clearly in the

Joseph story, as Joseph himself declares: "You intended to harm me, but God intended it for good to accomplish what is now being done, the saving of many lives" (Genesis 50:20).

And thus the Joseph story also functions as a foreshadowing, or a typology, of the story of Jesus. The point of comparison is not Joseph's innocence or perfection—Joseph exhibited neither of these. The point of comparison is that Joseph's story, just like the later narrative of Jesus, portrays for us a God who can take the worst that humans can do and turn it into an act of salvation.

Even those human actions directed against God's good purposes can be used to fulfill those very purposes. God's intentions toward us are always good, even when our intentions toward God are not. God can and will, if necessary, draw saving effects even out of acts of human evil. Joseph was rejected, sold into slavery, falsely accused, unjustly imprisoned, and then long forgotten—yet God used all that so that in the end Joseph could play the leading role in saving his family and many thousands of others besides. Jesus was misunderstood, rejected, abused, and finally crucified. He suffered the worst possible consequences of evil human intentions. Yet in the end Jesus emerged the victor, the savior of his own people, and of the entire world. Joseph's story foreshadowed that!

### DELIVERED IN ORDER TO BECOME A DELIVERER—MOSES

We turn our attention to the next OT faith hero, the next major character who abused his power yet became one of God's faithful servants, and another character foreshadowing Jesus and his ministry: Moses. As Genesis ends and Exodus begins, we read that about seventy people belonged to the slowly growing "people of God" (Genesis 46:27; Exodus 1:5). A mere four verses later (see Exodus 1:9) we read something astonishing. A new pharaoh, the most powerful man in the mightiest nation of that time and place, complains: "Look, the Israelite people are more numerous and more powerful than we" (NRSVue).

He was obviously exaggerating. If they had literally been stronger than the Egyptians, the Israelite people, who became enslaved by Egypt, simply would have walked away from their oppressors. No extraordinary redemptive miracle would have been needed to deliver them from slavery. But apparently their numbers had grown significantly in the intervening generations between verses 5 and 9. God's people had indeed become a large people group. God's plan had moved great strides forward; God's promise to Abraham was coming to pass. The Israelites were not yet literally as numerous as the stars of the heavens, but they were becoming a great nation.

But their growth was also their problem. Their hosts, the Egyptians, began to fear the growing power of the Hebrew people and reduced them to slavery. When that did not sufficiently reduce the strength and influence of the Hebrews, the Egyptians began to murder the baby boys and throw them into the Nile River (1:22). What was to become of God's great plan? It would have failed had God not intervened.

God saved the future deliverer, Moses, from impending death. Much later, God used Moses to deliver the entire nation. God's rescue act for baby Moses utilized the clever planning of a series of humans. God's rescue act for the entire nation included a whole series of miraculous interventions. With or without miracles, God will see that God's plans and purposes are fulfilled.

Some people stand out within their own generation. Moses, for example, was part of a generation where virtually all the male children were murdered (Exodus 1:22). In the next generation we find Joshua as unique among his peers. Virtually all adult males of his generation died in the wilderness. Only Joshua and Caleb made it all the way from Egypt into the promised land (Joshua 5:4; Numbers 14:21–24, 30). And then there is Jesus, rescued and protected by God while Herod murdered Bethlehem's innocent baby boys and Rachel wept for her children (Matthew 2:16–18). Do we see the pattern here? When God chooses a special servant for a unique rescue mission, God will often find ways to make them stand out among their peers, first by electing them and then by preserving them. Humans can create enormous havoc and grief, but amid humans' evil designs, God's plans and purposes will ultimately prevail.

The story of the salvation of baby Moses is one that most of us remember from Sunday school lessons (see Exodus 2:1–10). Moses had a clever and courageous mother willing to risk everything to save her son. First she took the risk of hiding the boy for three months. Then she risked floating him in a homemade boat on the mighty Nile, putting the baby's sister Miriam on the shore to keep watch. Perhaps she was well aware that Pharaoh's daughter went there to bathe. Perhaps she prayed that Pharaoh's daughter would find the baby and adopt him. Or perhaps the whole amazing story is simply one more example of God's astonishing and providential care for the one who would experience God's deliverance and then much later be used by God to deliver Israel.

When the princess found baby Moses, Miriam brilliantly proposed that the princess "hire" a nursing mother from the Israelites for the "unidentified child" found floating in the Nile. So Pharaoh's coffers paid Moses's birth mother to nurse her own boy, now protected by Egypt's most powerful family. When Moses was old enough, he was taken into and raised in Pharaoh's household.

Though Moses had been saved from Pharaoh's murderous hand, he himself became a murderer when he intervened in an interpersonal conflict and foolishly struck and killed an Egyptian. When the deed came to light, he fled the country to escape justice. Amazingly, he had not disqualified himself from being God's agent of deliverance. In fact, he had been taken into the wilderness to complete his training.

Growing up as a Hebrew in Pharaoh's household uniquely equipped Moses for the role God had designed for him. He was a Hebrew and he identified with his own people. Yet he was also adopted into the pharaoh's family. Thus he knew the language and culture of the Egyptians, and knew how to conduct himself in the corridors of power—not a bad set of skills for the one who would later be called to deliver the people of God from the power of the Egyptians. Now it was time to get the other half of the training he needed.

Moses still needed to learn to wait for God's timing. In Egypt he had jumped in with both feet the moment he spied injustice; he instinctively grabbed his sword, quite unaware that this was not how God intended to deliver the enslaved people. Moses would need to learn patience. And what better way to learn it than to spend decades as a shepherd learning to take good care of sheep—a skill he would later need in abundance when shepherding the people of God through the wilderness and leading them to greener pastures. Moses also needed to learn to recognize the presence and the voice of God. Sometimes that voice would be unmistakable (as at the burning bush). Sometimes it would be less obvious. Moses would also need to recognize when God was calling, challenging, and confronting Moses, recruiting him to lead the people of God (see 3:1–10).

Moses needed to learn that God would accept no excuses, no litany of feigned or genuine complaints about Moses's own incompetence. Moses needed to learn that the most effective servants of God are not those who think they can accomplish the task on their own, but those who know they need God's supernatural strength and the help of their brothers and sisters. Moses's biological brother and sister would later become co-leaders with him; later still, seventy others commissioned and empowered by God would take some of the leadership load off Moses's back (Numbers 11:16–17, 24–25).

## GOD'S MASTER PLAN

Most of all, Moses had to learn what God was really aiming to accomplish, what God's great plan was for the salvation of Israel and the whole world. No text in Scripture more transparently defines God's purposes for God's people than the text where God calls Moses to become their deliverer and leader:

> God also said to Moses, "I am the LORD. I appeared to Abraham, to Isaac and to Jacob as God Almighty, but by my name the LORD I did not make myself fully known to them. I also established my covenant with them to give them the land of Canaan, where they resided as foreigners. Moreover, I have heard the groaning of the Israelites, whom the Egyptians are enslaving, and I have remembered my covenant.
>
> "Therefore, say to the Israelites: 'I am the LORD, and I will bring you out from under the yoke of the Egyptians. I will free you from being slaves to them, and I will redeem you with an outstretched arm and with mighty acts of judgment. I will take you as my own people, and I will be your God. Then you will know that I am the LORD your God, who brought you out from under the yoke of the Egyptians. And I will bring you to the land I swore with uplifted

hand to give to Abraham, to Isaac and to Jacob. I will give it to you as a possession. I am the LORD.'" (Exodus 6:2–8)

God reveals a series of things to Moses:

- *God has a name: Yahweh (the LORD).* God is a personal God who wants to be in relationship with God's people. God's name means "I AM": I am there; I am there for you; I am the true God on whom you can depend (6:2).

- *God creates history.* This is the same God who appeared to Abraham, Isaac, and Jacob. This is the God who had set a plan in motion centuries before and who had guided the course of history through the intervening generations. In earlier generations God was known as "the Almighty." Now God comes as "the LORD," the one who will enter into a covenant relationship with Israel (6:3).

- *God has a good memory.* God had promised the ancestors of the presently enslaved Israelites a land of their own. And God had never forgotten that promise. Israel may have forgotten. Israel may have given up hope that the promise would ever be fulfilled. But God never forgets. God's earlier promise became part of a binding covenant, and God always fulfills covenant obligations. Moses will lead Israel out of Egypt and on a journey to the land that God promised Abraham's descendants (6:4–5).

- *God loves mercy and justice.* God does not sit idly by when humans enslave humans, when justice is sacrificed on the altars of power and privilege. When injustice rules, God knows and cares. God sometimes sends coworkers to stand alongside the victims of injustice and to work for peace. God always suffers with those who are abused—until the day comes when the tables are turned (6:5). Then God intervenes.

- *God rescues and saves.* God normally respects human free choice, even those choices freely made to oppose God and God's people, even those choices that produce injustice and evil. At some point, however, God says, "Enough is enough!" and redeems God's people (6:6).
- *God covenants with a people group.* The fullness of God's plan is not centered around private relationships between God and individuals. God has elected a people and will be that people's God (6:7). God's plan is to save, accompany, shape, and then use this people group to provide salvation for all the peoples of the earth.
- *God promises future revelation.* What an incredible promise that Moses "will know" God (6:7). God will not only rescue and deliver. God will show up! God will live among those who acknowledge God. At the very moment Moses hears these words, the promise is being kept. But God is also promising future revelation. God and God's ways will be revealed through acts of divine guidance, through prophetic words, through tablets of stone, through covenant documents and other holy writings. God has many ways to reveal both God's person and God's plans. When God's people experience God's deliverance, they will know that God is God!
- *God gives life.* "The land" was not merely a geographic location (6:8). Land meant life and freedom and abundance. It would be a great blessing to live in the promised land. But it would also be an assignment, a mission. Israel was to live in the land openly and in plain sight of all the other nations so that others would see what it means to experience God's blessing and live in faithful covenant partnership with God. Israel would be a visible

demonstration of real life, of shalom, of God's creative hand again making things "very good."

What a calling! Can anyone live up to a calling like that? Would Israel be able to do all that God had planned for them? Not as long as they were still groaning under slavery to the Egyptians.

## THE EXODUS FROM EGYPT

The rescue of Israel from Egypt literally happened overnight, but the preparations for God's deliverance took place over a far longer time. Moses and his brother Aaron confronted Pharaoh with the demand: "Let my people go!" (Exodus 5:1). After extensive (and sometimes deceitful) negotiations (see 5:3), numerous severe plagues, and many broken promises on the part of the pharaoh, it was time for the final showdown. God announced that Pharaoh and his fellow oppressors would be judged, and the people of God would be set free.

Israel was instructed to prepare for the first Passover—a feast celebrating deliverance. The main dish would be a lamb, a sacrificial lamb, whose blood would be smeared on the door-posts. God promised Israel: "The blood will be a sign for you on the houses where you are, and when I see the blood, I will pass over you. No destructive plague will touch you when I strike Egypt" (12:13).

God's angel of death would visit those houses without the blood of the sacrifice on the doorposts (that is, Egyptian homes), and those households would lose their firstborn son.

When God finally came in judgment, the reactions came swiftly. "During the night Pharaoh summoned Moses and Aaron and said, 'Up! Leave my people, you and the Israelites! Go, worship the LORD as you have requested'" (12:31).

And so the Israelites escaped Egypt and their slavery there. Yet once again Pharaoh reneged on his word. He sent the entire Egyptian army after the fleeing Israelites. This time God really did say, "Enough is enough!" God opened up the sea to allow the Israelites to pass through in safety, and then shut the sea to drown the pursuing army.

We may be uncertain about how to interpret these narratives. God is indeed a miracle-working God, yet the authors of these texts were not dispassionate historians. They were aiming for more than merely recalling the details, for saying "exactly what happened." Their goal was to demonstrate that the exodus was an act of God. We cannot know what other factors were at play. What demonic forces were at work? Which palace intrigues divided or weakened the pharaoh's power? To what extent did the superstitions of the Egyptians play a role?

As already noted, when baby Moses was delivered from Pharaoh's murderous hand, God's intervention was a combination of human factors and divine activity. This combination is common in Scripture. Miracles are often reported simply as miracles without parsing out how interacting "natural," "human," and "supernatural" factors may have contributed to the final outcome. The whole event of Israel's exodus from Egypt shows evidence of spiritual warfare, of divine judgment, and of so-called natural phenomena (such as God sending a "strong east wind"; 14:21). We will never know whether the whole exodus experience seemed obviously supernatural all along the way to every observer. But looking back later, it was clear to the Israelites: God delivered Israel from Egyptian slavery. It was a mighty miracle.[1]

The texts also illustrate that in the exodus, God defeated not only the Egyptians but also supernatural powers of evil.

More was happening here than a contest between Moses and Pharaoh, more than political maneuverings of two people groups, more than social unrest in master/slave relations, more than ethnic conflict, more than social rebellion. This was also cosmic warfare, a spiritual battle.

At the beginning of the biblical story, God's archenemy appeared in the guise of a snake. In Egypt, God's enemy worked through systems of injustice and abuse of power. The Bible speaks of principalities and powers, quasi-spiritual realities embedded in evil systems that practice injustice and abuse power. It is not insignificant that Pharaoh summoned "the wise men and sorcerers, and the Egyptian magicians" (7:11). Just as God has coworkers, people called to join in God's work, so also the enemy recruits humans to work diabolical evil. Here we see Pharaoh and his sorcerers trying to destroy God's plan for Israel and thus for the salvation of the whole world.

God's act of deliverance on Israel's behalf was God's guarantee that the grand strategy God had begun for the salvation of the world would not be jeopardized. The power of evil is great, but never great enough to prevent what God aims to accomplish. But the converse of this is also illustrated here. Wherever God is at work, intervening in human affairs to redeem and restore, we can be sure that evil opponents, whether human or supernatural, will stir up resistance. Evil will not destroy God's good plans; but neither will God's good plans move forward unchallenged.

The exodus story assures us that God is always, in the end, the victor, more powerful than any opponents. God is always ready, willing, and able to bring about justice where injustice seems to rule. This is what the Hebrews were acknowledging when they sang in jubilation, "The LORD is a warrior; the LORD is his name. . . . Your right hand, LORD, was majestic in power. Your right hand, LORD, shattered the enemy. . . . Sing to the LORD, for he is highly exalted. Both horse and driver he has hurled into the sea" (15:3, 6, 21).

A host of enslaved people had just been set free. They were to become God's covenant people, a redeemed community, a model society living out God's justice and shalom. God would enter into a covenant relationship with Israel, would demonstrate faithfulness to them, would challenge them to be faithful to the covenant in return. And God would reveal to all of Israel what God had already revealed to their leader Moses: God is a personal God with a name; God is merciful; and God works justice, cares for, and leads the covenant people. God is the God of history forming Israel into a people that can shape history as God's coworkers. And God will shower on Israel abundant life, if only Israel will follow God's call and God's voice.

## WHAT CAN WE LEARN FROM GENESIS 37–EXODUS 15?

The "Egypt chapters" in the long story of God's people provide very important teaching for the Christian church. We should view these chapters as windows into the way that Israel's God, Yahweh, whom we know more fully through Jesus as Father, Son, and Spirit, remains faithful through thick and thin, regardless of what humans do. These chapters reveal important aspects of God's nature, God's purposes, and God's way of relating to God's covenant people. These chapters tell us a great deal about our *own* history, for we are now the heirs of God's promises to Israel. These stories are our stories. We can say along with any ethnic Jew: "We were slaves in Egypt, but God set us free!"

# Questions for discussion

1. When you consider the dysfunctional families in the first three generations of the formation of Israel, what does that reveal about the faithfulness and the ingenuity of God, who works out divine purposes despite all our human failures and shortcomings?

2. "You intended to harm me, but God intended it for good to accomplish what is now being done, the saving of many lives" (Genesis 50:20). This principle is illustrated in the story of Joseph. Where have you experienced that God has transformed evil acts and intentions into something good?

3. "Miracles are often reported simply as miracles without parsing out how interacting 'natural,' 'human,' and 'supernatural' factors may have contributed to the final outcome." "With or without miracles, God will see that God's plans and purposes are fulfilled." Where have you experienced God's intervention, whether with or without great miracles?

# GOD, THE COVENANT KEEPER

### (Exodus 16–20)

*Do not think that I have come to abolish the Law or the Prophets; I have not come to abolish them but to fulfill them.*
*—Matthew 5:17*

In Jesus' day, some Bible teachers focused on rules and regulations, commands and prohibitions, dos and don'ts, as if these were at the very center of God's priorities for the people of God. That was how they read their Bible. And Jesus challenged that way of reading the Scriptures over and over again.

Given that, isn't it astonishing that so many Christians seem to agree more with Jesus' opponents than they do with Jesus on this question? They seem convinced that the Old Testament is mostly about law, and that "grace and truth" are introduced into the equation by Jesus. So "good riddance," Old Testament! We are people of the new covenant!

But if Jesus is the center of our faith, then Jesus' challenge to his religious contemporaries means he still challenges that way of reading of the Old Testament. That is very much what this chapter is all about.

❖

A covenant requires two parties. In the case of the covenant that God made with Israel, the two parties are Yahweh, creator and Lord of heaven and earth, and Israel, the set-apart people group that God had been bringing into existence. God had chosen Abraham. God had put a special call on his life to be both blessed and a blessing. He would be the father of a great nation. And God planned that through that nation, salvation would be made available to the whole world.

In time, Isaac, the promised son of the aged Abraham and Sarah, inherited the blessing and the mission. It was then passed on not through Isaac's older son, Esau, but through his younger son, Jacob. Jacob in turn, along with his two wives and two concubines, produced twelve sons and at least one daughter. At last Abraham's family began to grow. Soon we read of seventy and then of thousands. Jacob's sons produced families, family clans, and finally tribes. Ultimately, twelve tribes (or thirteen, depending on how one counts them!), though in many ways still quite independent, formed one large people group and finally a nation, the people of Israel.

This people group descended physically from Grandfather Abraham. Yet God tried to make clear right from the start that "birth from Abraham" was a secondary feature of this people group. More important than physical descent was the covenant that the God of Abraham, Isaac, and Jacob was making with them. That would be the defining characteristic of this people group.

Blood relationships can be a strong force that binds people together. Other factors supplement this—a common history, a distinctive language or dialect, unique habits and customs, and so much more. All these define a multitude of people as an identifiable people group, a cultural entity, an ethnic group.

But all these factors put together cannot bring into existence "God's people." God's great strategy for saving humanity could not reach its goal through an ethnic people group. God needed a community of faith and faithfulness. God's plan was to create a people held together by ties stronger than any ethnic ties. Israel was to be held together by a common commitment to live in relationship with the one true God. God wanted a "holy" people, a people set apart from all other peoples on the earth. God created a brand-new one and created it on a brand-new basis.

God provided an aged couple with a miracle child. God provided a substitute sacrifice that preserved that boy's life. God protected and blessed Jacob, despite all his underhandedness and deceit. God used Joseph to rescue the whole family of Jacob from starvation. This list could be multiplied many times.

Hundreds of years later, this one family clan had become a very large nation. Then God intervened powerfully again, rescuing them from slavery and from the pursuing army of Egypt. And so, many miracles later, here they were, thousands of formerly enslaved persons camped in the Sinai Desert. What now? Well, the first order of business was to celebrate! And after that, God set the agenda: All of Israel would be formed into God's covenant partner—the chosen people!

## GOD IS A WARRIOR

Moses was the first to lead the people in celebrations. Then Miriam and Aaron enlarged the music team. All Israel joined in worship, jubilant and praising God for the mighty miracles that had given them their liberty.

> I will sing to the LORD,
>> for he is highly exalted.
> Both horse and driver
>> he has hurled into the sea.
> The LORD is my strength and my defense;
>> he has become my salvation.
> He is my God, and I will praise him,
>> my father's God, and I will exalt him.
> The LORD is a warrior;
>> the LORD is his name. . . .
>
> Sing to the LORD,
>> for he is highly exalted.
> Both horse and driver
>> he has hurled into the sea.
> (Exodus 15:1–3, 21)

The Israelites knew: their newfound freedom was something *God* had given them. Humans may have contributed to the process, but it was ultimately the mighty hand of God, the very God of their ancestors Abraham, Isaac, and Jacob, that rescued them from Egypt. God is the redeemer. God is the warrior. God is Lord and Yahweh is God's name. Note how God models here what God will later demand of those who lead God's people: "May he defend the afflicted among the people and save the children of the needy; may he crush the oppressor" (Psalm 72:4).

In chapter 9 of this book, we will address the larger problem of war in the Old Testament and the extermination of whole people groups. Let me be clear: What happened when

God rescued Israel from Egypt has little or nothing to do with what modern states aim to do when they declare war on each other. These chapters in Exodus are not about God justifying Israel's military ambitions. God is the warrior here. God is the one fighting on behalf of a chosen and oppressed people. This is about God creating justice for the downtrodden, not about nations securing their borders and their privileges.

Israel knew how to celebrate. A Jewish friend of mine once summarized the meaning of all Jewish festivals like this: "They tried to kill us. God rescued us. Let's eat!" I suppose Moses and Miriam might have worded it like this: "We were slaves. God rescued us. Let's sing and dance!" That's not a bad model for us when we have experienced the goodness of God.

## GOD'S ELECTION IS GRACE

God wanted Israel to respond with a commitment of faithfulness to God for all that God had done. God had chosen Israel as an act of grace. Not only Israel needed to understand this—so do we! Otherwise, we stand in danger of reading the whole Old Testament from the wrong perspective.

Israel had not earned its election. Whenever Israel thought they could somehow earn God's favor, a lot of things went wrong. In one text, God formulates the whole matter like this:

> You are a people holy to the LORD your God. The LORD your God has chosen you out of all the peoples on the face of the earth to be his people, his treasured possession. The LORD did not set his affection on you and choose you because you were more numerous than other peoples, for you were the fewest of all peoples. But it was because the LORD loved you and kept the oath he swore to your ancestors that he brought you out with a mighty hand and redeemed

you from the land of slavery, from the power of Pharaoh
king of Egypt. Know therefore that the LORD your God is
God; he is the faithful God, keeping his covenant of love to
a thousand generations of those who love him and keep his
commandments. (Deuteronomy 7:6–9)

Whatever blessings Israel experiences will be because God
is gracious, not because Israel is deserving. Whatever blessings
other nations will experience through Israel will be because
God is at work, not because Israel is so successful.

Here we see principles at work that pervade the entire
Bible. God calls out people for a specific mission. Yet the call
is never because these people have become so special, so effective, so promising. The call is God's free choice, an expression
of grace. God often chooses not the strong, but the weak. God
wants to make sure nobody ever reaches the conclusion that
divine favor can be earned or divine goals achieved by human
effort alone.

The Gideon story in the book of Judges illustrates this well.
As Gideon is about to go to war with his powerful army, God
stops him in his tracks with an astonishing announcement:
"You have too many men. I cannot deliver Midian into their
hands, or Israel would boast against me, 'My own strength has
saved me'" (7:2). The apostle Paul later picks up on that same
principle. Finding himself hard-pressed, perplexed, persecuted,
struck down (see 2 Corinthians 4:8–9), Paul confesses: "We
have this treasure in jars of clay to show that this all-surpassing
power is from God and not from us" (4:7). God is much more
interested in working through our weakness than through our
strength, for then it can be seen that God is at work.

Throughout Scripture the point is emphasized: "'Not
by might nor by power, but by my Spirit,' says the LORD

Almighty" (Zechariah 4:6). "My grace is sufficient for you, for my power is made perfect in weakness" (2 Corinthians 12:9). Just as Gideon's army needed to be small to demonstrate that the victory belonged to the Lord, so the church of Jesus Christ must recognize its weakness if it is to demonstrate the Lord's strength.

Israel often viewed its election as a special possession, a privilege given only to them. Even the story of God's covenant-making at Sinai was sometimes retold as if it were a story of Israel's achievement and not of God's grace. Instead of remembering that "the LORD did not set his affection on you and choose you because you were more numerous than other peoples, for you were the fewest of all peoples" (Deuteronomy 7:7), they imagined that God had selected the most deserving nation of them all . . . as if the offer had gone out to all nations, and only Israel had been righteous enough to be God's covenant partner.

The Bible teaches the opposite. Israel could not earn, and did not need to earn, the right to be God's people. Nobody ever does or ever can. Covenant partnership is always by God's grace. Israel was a "chosen people," and that is something completely different from being a deserving people.

## GRACE COMES BEFORE LAW

Election is always by grace. But then what is the role of law? The law came after election, and the law must always play a subordinate role within God's plans and purposes. Grace is the basis for creation, election, and covenant partnership. Law is the basis for none of these.

Some Christians may no doubt respond with astonishment or skepticism: Wasn't the covenant that God made with Israel a covenant of law? Didn't grace begin with the New

Testament, with the new covenant that God makes with us? As widespread as this view seems to be, it has little basis in Scripture. We love to quote John 1:17: "The law was given through Moses; grace and truth came through Jesus Christ." But the New Testament insists that Jesus did not come to replace law with grace. Jesus himself said, "Do not think that I have come to abolish the Law or the Prophets; I have not come to abolish them but to fulfill them" (Matthew 5:17).

Grace and truth did indeed come through Jesus. Jesus is indeed the one in whom all grace and truth find their fullest embodiment. But neither grace nor truth *began* with Jesus. Grace was the basis for the creation of the world. Grace was the basis for covenant-making. In worship, Israel repeatedly affirmed that God's grace endures forever (Psalm 136). Grace (*hesed* in Hebrew, also translated mercy, loving-kindness, covenant faithfulness) is the driving force of the entire Old Testament and of the New.

What, then, is the role of the law? Throughout the ages, some have wrongly supposed that the law is the basis for earning eternal life. No doubt some Jews in the Old Testament and during Jesus' lifetime thought this as well—though not nearly as many Jews have believed this as Christians often suppose! This view is not what the Old Testament teaches. Jesus and, later, the apostle Paul put great effort into clarifying the real purpose of God's law. It was never intended to earn God's favor. Any who have ever believed this have been wrong.

Others have wrongly supposed that the only valid function of the law is to demonstrate how incapable we are of living according to its demands, and thus to drive us to quit trying and choose repentance instead of obedience. Law can and does sometimes have that effect (see Romans 7:7), but it has many other purposes and functions as well.

To understand the subordinate role of law within God's covenant plan, we do well to look closely at the events surrounding God's covenant-making with Israel at Mount Sinai. The texts reveal that covenant-making is about relationship and about allegiance; it is not about law-keeping.

Perhaps the clearest evidence of this is Exodus 19:4–6. Ask Christians what they would find if they turned to Exodus 20, and most respond immediately: the Ten Commandments. Ask them what they would find if they turned to Exodus 19, and they would have no idea. What a travesty! Exodus 19 is far more central to God's plan than Exodus 20. This is how God addresses Israel:

> You yourselves have seen what I did to Egypt, and how I carried you on eagles' wings and brought you to myself. Now if you obey me fully and keep my covenant, then out of all nations you will be my treasured possession. Although the whole earth is mine, you will be for me a kingdom of priests and a holy nation. (19:4–6)

Here is Israel, or perhaps we should say here is a chaotic mob of people newly emancipated from slavery. God wants to make a binding covenant with them. This will not be a covenant of law! This will be a binding personal relationship between God and the people. Each party will commit to be loyal to the other. As both parties faithfully carry out their commitment (God always being more faithful than Israel could ever be!), God will use Israel for the mission that God has always had in mind. Israel will be that set-apart nation which benefits all nations by demonstrating the blessings of living in relationship with God. Israel will be that priestly kingdom, that mediating nation, through whom the nations can bring their offerings to God and in turn hear the pronouncement of God's gracious forgiveness.

We so readily associate the Sinai covenant with law. Why then does the key Exodus 19 passage talk about everything but law?

"You yourselves have seen what I did to Egypt, and how I carried you on eagles' wings and brought you to"—to what? To the place of lawgiving? No! "I brought you to myself." The covenant that God is making is not first and foremost about law, or obedience, or accountability, or judgment, or vindication. It is not first and foremost about earthly benefits. God freed Israel from slavery to establish a deep, abiding, and personal relationship between God and God's people. God was not looking for Israel's efforts to be obedient. God was looking for Israel's heart! This was to become a relationship of mutual loyalty and love. God's purpose from the very beginning of creation had remained God's purpose through the long history of election and bringing into existence the people of Israel. Now that would be sealed in the covenant which God was making with Israel at Sinai. As an eagle protects its young, so God had protected a vulnerable people and led them to freedom. Now the time had come to seal a covenant of love and faithfulness with them.

"Now if you obey"—obey what? Obey laws? No! "Obey me fully." Actually, the text is not exactly about obeying, and we certainly should not read commandments into this line. Israel is not (yet) called to obey laws; Israel is called to listen to God! A more literal translation would be "Now if you listen to my voice." Later, God will give universal commandments—what we call the Ten Commandments—about what is to be done and avoided.

God's plan was never to lead Israel only through universal laws. God's plan was to keep speaking to them, guiding them, instructing them along the journey. Sometimes God's leading would be very clear—visible, audible. Sometimes it would be less clear. God would speak through Moses, through prophets. God would lead through pillars of cloud and fire, through circumstances, through special revelations. Israel was called to listen for God's voice, not the voice of a lawgiver and judge, but the voice of a leader, guide, and companion.

"Now if you listen to my voice and keep my"—my what? My rules? My laws? My commandments? Still not yet. God's call is to "keep my covenant." God is more interested in loyalty and faithfulness than meticulous observance of rules. Indeed, when rules and commandments become central in a relationship, loyalty and love no longer have room to flourish.

Yes, there will be rules and guidelines, commands and prohibitions. But God first wants to make perfectly clear that this covenant will be based mostly on what God is doing, not on what Israel does. By grace God created; by grace God elected; by grace God redeemed; now by grace God will establish a covenant relationship. God acts first; everything Israel does will be a response. Before God lays any covenant demands on Israel, God declares: "Out of all nations you will be my treasured possession. Although [the word could also be translated *because*] the whole earth is mine, you will be for me a kingdom of priests and a holy nation" (Exodus 19:5–6).

Note well: Though this is a covenant between God and Israel, it is for the sake of the whole world. God is Israel's Lord, but God is also the Lord of all the earth. Israel will be a priestly kingdom. That does not mean that Israel will be a nation with a large and well-functioning priesthood. Israel *as an entire nation* will play a priestly role in this world. Israel will mediate the gap between humanity and God. That is what priests do. Within Israel, the priests representatively led Israel into God's presence and on God's behalf pronounced blessing and forgiveness on Israel. Priests are there for the benefit of those who are not priests. Priests are intermediaries between God and the rest of the people. And Israel as God's priestly nation is intermediary between God and humanity.

Israel must be set apart from all the other peoples to play that crucial mediating role. Israel must be a holy people (the word means set apart; distinct) so that all the others can observe what happens when a people lives in covenant with creator God. Israel must represent for the whole world what God originally intended for all humanity, what God established in the garden of Eden, what God will one day reestablish in the city of God. Israel will never do it perfectly, and therefore God's grace and forgiveness will always be needed. But Israel has a mission, a priestly role, on behalf of God and the nations. Grasping this allows us to understand the subordinate role of law in God's covenant-making.

## THE LAW OUTLINES COVENANT FAITHFULNESS

The law is a very broad concept in the Old Testament. The Hebrew word is *tôrâ*, and it includes not only commands and prohibitions but many other guidelines for life. Part of this focuses on the ethical requirements Israel was to live by, centered in the Ten Commandments. But torah is broader than ethics. Law includes detailed instructions for carrying out religious worship; it includes rules for hygiene and for farming practice; it includes social institutions designed to prevent poverty and the unjust accumulation for wealth or power. Law is much more than commands and prohibitions. For now, we will focus in a general way on law, leaving for chapter 10 further discussion of some of the details and of Christian obligations in relation to them.

Law was never intended to be the center of the covenant, yet law does play a significant role within it. That is seen in the connection between the covenant-making and lawgiving that happen together at Mount Sinai (Exodus 19–20). This is not a temporary connection that disappears with the arrival of Jesus. That claim is sometimes made by Christians and then defended by verses like "The law was our guardian until Christ came that we might be justified by faith" (Galatians 3:24).

This text emphatically does not mean that law was the central feature of the covenant with Israel and that it was replaced by faith after Jesus established the new covenant. Such an interpretation contradicts the apostle Paul's main point in his letter to the Galatians. Paul argues that it is not law that stood at the center of the Old Testament but rather promise (see Galatians 3:15–18). He also argues that the covenant that God made with Abraham was a covenant of grace and of faith, and that this covenant stayed in force even when the law was given later, since the law on its own could never have made people righteous.

God's righteousness becomes ours not through the law but rather through believers holding fast to the promises of God in *faith* and *faithfulness* (the New Testament uses only one word for both of these!). Just like OT believers, NT believers are made righteous not through law, but through faith. And that is why Abraham is also *our* father in the faith.

The primary function of law in the Old Testament was to help people understand what it looked like to live in covenant faithfulness to God. The central concern is always relationship: a relationship with God, and relationships in the community of faith. The very content of the Ten Commandments themselves reveals this. The first part clarifies that Yahweh alone is the one true God and that therefore our worship belongs to this God alone. The second part specifies how people within the community of faith live when they are bound together in a covenant relationship with this one God. They live in a life-giving community that does not kill, steal, or deceive, does not commit adultery or envy others for what they have.

Jesus came to fulfill the law. Jesus lived in precisely the way that God had intended all the people of God to live. Only Jesus has ever succeeded in fully demonstrating what complete covenant faithfulness in relation to God and others in the covenant community looks like. His perfect obedience qualified him to be our representative before God, our human-divine High Priest, the one who alone can bring our sacrifices and worship into God's presence and speak God's forgiveness for our failures.

Yes, we are called to fulfill God's law. And no, we cannot do it perfectly. That is the paradox of the life of faith. For all our failures and sins, we are offered forgiveness. Covenant relationship depends not on law-keeping and human achievement but on God's gracious initiative and covenant mercy. That is true today in what we call the new covenant. That was also true at Mount Sinai in what we call the old covenant. The main change is that Israel's faith in God's mercy expressed itself through a system of sacrifices and priestly ministry. Our faith in God's mercy expresses itself in trusting Jesus Christ and his faithfulness so that our sins can be forgiven. Then as now, Yahweh our God remains true and faithful in a covenant that centers on relationship, loyalty, and grace.

At Sinai, Israel entered into a binding obligation of covenant loyalty to God. They obligated themselves to live by the covenant stipulations. And to what did God commit as the greater party in this covenant agreement? I quote Bernhard Ott's summary:

Since God is a good Lord and King, three incredible promises are immediately pronounced:

1. Your security and freedom are my responsibility: I will go to battle on your behalf.
2. Your daily provisions are my responsibility: I will take care of all your needs.
3. Your journey is my responsibility: I will be your leader.[1]

Jesus spoke similarly to his followers: "Your heavenly Father knows that you need them [things like food and clothing]. But seek first his kingdom and his righteousness, and all these things will be given to you as well" (Matthew 6:32–33).

Some Bible interpreters draw a very thick line between the Old Testament and the New, at least in terms of their understanding of salvation. I see that quite differently. Then and now, our relationship with God is dependent entirely on these realities:

- that God offers true life to individuals and to people groups;
- that we are invited to receive it freely, as a gift from a generous God;
- that the covenant relationship always remains central; and
- that the law plays a subordinate role.

Then as now the law reveals what it looks like when we, in gratitude to God, show by our obedience that we are serious about the relationship God offers us, that we trust God to guide us with commands and prohibitions toward a rich and full life, and that we are committed to living in ways that please God.

There has been significant revision along the way in terms of the precise content of the law by which we are to live. For example, we are not required to live by the food laws that applied to OT Israel. Many of the laws that governed the communal life of Israel as a nation-state do not apply to the multiethnic, transnational body of Christ we call the church. In general, law still plays the same role today that it did for ancient Israel. It guides us to worship God aright, to live faithfully and justly in community, and to represent God and God's ways in a world not yet redeemed.

So what has changed significantly from OT times until today? In some ways, not all that much, and in other ways, a great deal. The main shift is that God has personally come down in the person of Jesus Christ to embody visibly on earth all that the covenant involves. Israel looked forward in faith to a coming redeemer. We look back in gratitude to God for coming in person to be that redeemer. Israel, at the best of times, understood its role as a priestly one on behalf of all the nations on earth. We, at the best of times, recognize that our deepest loyalties are not to our tribe or our ethnicity, our culture or our nation, but to the Creator and Redeemer, and to the worldwide body of Christ that lives in covenant with this God. And our primary mission is to be the light on the hill that draws all humanity back to God.

One more important thing has changed! God's covenant with Israel was written on tablets of stone (Exodus 24:12). Now God's law is written on our hearts (Jeremiah 31:33; Hebrews 8:10). The law is not so much an external standard that calls us to faithfulness as it is an inner desire to do so. That change happened because God's very Spirit has come to live within us. The experience of Spirit-anointing, of Spirit-empowerment, was once reserved for a small minority called out from among the Israelites to be mediators between God and God's people. Now it is the experience of all God's people. And so a great deal that Israel could only long for, we can now experience. Yes, a great deal has changed. But it would be a great mistake to oversimplify what has happened to saying that Israel lived by law, and we now live by grace.

## WHAT IS SO IMPORTANT FOR US IN EXODUS 16–20?

What should motivate Christians to pay close attention to the old covenant that God made with Israel way back at Mount Sinai? The new covenant that is ours through Jesus Christ is not a brand-new covenant replacing one that had become obsolete. The new covenant is a continuation, a fulfillment, an expansion, a deepening of a covenant that God has always made with God's called-out people. The church is not a replacement for Israel. The church is incorporated into Israel through Jesus, and this happens in a way that makes transparent God's intention from the start: God's people are defined not by ethnic, racial, cultural, or national identity markers, but by the grace of God freely given and gratefully received in a covenant of faith and faithfulness.

## *Questions for discussion*

1.  "God's righteousness becomes ours not through
    the law but rather through believers holding fast to
    the promises of God in *faith* and *faithfulness* (the
    New Testament uses only one word for both of
    these!). Just like OT believers, NT believers are made
    righteous not through law, but rather through faith.
    And that is why Abraham is also *our* father in the
    faith." What is your response to the claim that this
    understanding of righteousness not only applies to
    believers in the New Testament, but already applied
    to Israel in the Old?

2.  "Jesus came to fulfill the law. Jesus lived in precisely
    the way that God had intended all the people of
    God to live. Only Jesus has ever succeeded in fully
    demonstrating what complete covenant faithfulness
    in relation to God and others in the covenant com-
    munity looks like." What implications does this have
    for those who follow Jesus?

3.  "The new covenant that is ours through Jesus Christ
    is not a brand-new covenant replacing one that had
    become obsolete. The new covenant is a continu-
    ation, a fulfillment, an expansion, a deepening of
    a covenant that God has always made with God's
    called-out people." How does this perspective help us
    embrace the unity of the two Testaments that make
    up the Christian Bible?

# GOD'S PEOPLE IN THE OLD TESTAMENT AND IN THE NEW TESTAMENT

*I have other sheep that are not of this sheep pen. I must bring them also. They too will listen to my voice, and there shall be one flock and one shepherd. —John 10:16*

One flock! One shepherd! Yet many Bible readers seem to think that God has more than one flock . . . a Jewish one and a Gentile one. Or that God once had a Jewish flock, but then swapped it out for a Gentile flock. And many are also quite unclear what the defining characteristics of "flock membership" are.

*Flock* is only one of many metaphors for the people of God. This chapter examines some of the basic vocabulary used to speak of God's people in the Old Testament (in the Hebrew language) and in the New Testament (in Greek). We will explore in more depth the issue of how "Israel" is related to "the church." The whole matter is of utmost importance if we want to claim that the first three-quarters of our Bible are really and truly part of authoritative Scripture for the church.

❖

In the previous chapter we examined Exodus 19:4–6, where God declares that Israel was God's special possession, God's elect people, God's holy nation. The word *holy* does not mean that Israel had reached some high level of moral perfection. The word has nothing to do with achievement. At its core it is not about moral superiority at all. To be holy is to be *set apart*, it is to be *distinct*. Israel was set apart by God and for God; Israel was distinct from all other people groups, called to live by a different set of standards. The whole earth belongs to God; all the nations are God's; yet Israel is a special possession, set apart, unique, called to live differently from all the others. The setting apart of Israel from all the others represented God's new strategy for reaching all the others.

### ETHNOS AND LAOS

We now turn to a second text narrating how God called Israel to be God's covenant partner, God's holy, set-apart people. It comes from a text parallel to Exodus 19, Deuteronomy's retelling of the Sinai event. (In Greek, Deuteronomy means "second law/torah.") Here Moses, in his parting words, clarifies what the people of Israel got themselves into when they became God's covenant partners.

> You have declared this day that the LORD is your God and that you will walk in obedience to him, that you will keep his decrees, commands and laws—that you will listen to him. And the LORD has declared this day that you are his

people, his treasured possession as he promised, and that you are to keep all his commands. He has declared that he will set you in praise, fame and honor high above all the nations he has made and that you will be a people holy to the LORD your God, as he promised. (Deuteronomy 26:17–19)

It is not always clear from English translations that the original Hebrew text uses two different words to designate people / people groups / nations. The first word is *am*, and it is used in Deuteronomy 26:18, where God declares that Israel is "his people," and then again in the next verse, where Israel is designated as "a people holy." The second word is *goy* (plural *goiim*). It is used to designate all the people groups—"all the nations" (26:19). Israel is one of those *goiim*, but because Israel is not like all the others, it is designated as God's *am*, God's *am kadosh* (God's set-apart people group). In this context, *am* means something more like "fellowship" or "faith community."

The difference is carefully preserved in the Greek translation (known as the Septuagint and abbreviated LXX) of this originally Hebrew text. The Greek text influenced how NT writers, writing in Greek, referred to God's covenant people group, the church. The two Greek words are *ethnos* and *laos*. Every nation, every people group on earth, is an *ethnos*. But the one *ethnos* that is set apart, Israel, is designated as God's *laos* (26:18). Israel is one of the *ethnē*, but because Israel is not like all the others, it is designated as God's *laos*, God's *laos hagios* (God's set-apart people group; 26:19).

Even though Israel is an *ethnos*, an ethnic people group, no more and no less than all the other ethnic groups (*ethnē*) on earth, Israel's deepest identity is not its ethnic identity, but its identity as God's *laos*. When speaking of God's NT people group, NT authors like Paul and Peter connect the church not to Israel's ethnicity, but to Israel's status as God's *laos*. The church is designated either as God's "set-apart *ethnos*" or, far more often, as God's *laos* (see especially 1 Peter 2:9–10). And the New Testament reveals that the original assignment which God had given Israel is now the primary role of the church. "I have made you a light for Gentiles [*ethnē* in Greek], that you may bring salvation to the ends of the earth" (Acts 13:47; Paul is quoting Isaiah 49:6).

The holy nation, God's set-apart people in OT times (Israel), finds its continuation in the NT church. But that continuity is a *laos* continuity, not an *ethnos* continuity. In other words, Israel's status as God's faith community finds its continuity in the church. But in terms of the ethnic makeup of God's people group, a great deal changes in the New Testament. Now the members of the church represent every *ethnos* on earth.

At this point, many Christians protest: But how can we be the continuation of Israel; we are not Jews! My first response is that, actually, many of us are Jews! The church of Jesus Christ has among its members many Jews, many Arabs, many Japanese, many Swiss, many Paraguayans, many Inuit. To be ethnically Jewish (or not) is one thing; to be a member of the body of Christ is another thing entirely. The more clearly we can see this distinction, the more clearly we will also be able to understand the relationship between *ethnos* and *laos* in Scripture.

What the New Testament emphasizes (though this was already evident in the Old Testament) is that to be ethnically Jewish and to be a member of God's covenant people group are never identical concepts, no matter how much or how little overlap there is between those who are the one and those who are the other. From the time of Abraham until several decades after Pentecost, God's covenant people group con-sisted primarily of those with Jewish ethnicity. Since then, it has expanded to include representatives of virtually every people group on earth.

The church has now incorporated many ethnicities into the one *laos* of God. The church is the same *laos* of God that Israel had been called to be. That *laos* was, in OT times, *centered* in Israel, but was never *identical* with it. Today it is centered around Jesus. Through covenant partnership with God, we have become members of the household of Israel, not the eth-nic household, but rather the covenant community. After Pen-tecost, this household spread from its Jewish roots to become a global, multiethnic family of faith.

An *ethnos*, as can be seen from the English words we derive from it, speaks of *ethnic* identity. An ethnic people group (*goy* in Hebrew; *ethnos* in Greek) is defined by its distinctive ethnic features—a common language and history, common habits and customs, favorite dishes, music, dance, and so on. People who share a distinctive ethnicity tend to look at the world in similar ways, to interpret their own history and identity in similar ways, and easily recognize who does and does not belong to their ethnic group.

The Hebrew word *am* and the Greek word *laos* function very differently. The biblical concept of God's *laos* begins with Abraham. Abraham would be the father of a *goy*, an *ethnos*. But God insisted right from the start: This will be a set-apart kind of *ethnos* so that it can be God's *laos*. Abraham was called away from his homeland, called to go to a new place to begin a new people group. The break with the past symbolized a new identity as *laos*—that is, more than merely *ethnos*. This people group came into being not as all others do, but through election, through call, through God's miraculous interventions.

Israel developed its own ethnic and cultural identity. But Israel was reminded over and over again, by its Scriptures and by its prophets, that Israel was to be different from its neighbors and to be God's *laos*. They would be the people of Israel, to be sure, but they would also be the people of God. They would form a nation, to be sure, but they would also be God's faithful covenant community. From the start, Israel was both an *ethnos* and a *laos*. The problem comes when people confuse the one with the other.

God did not say to Israel: "If you speak Hebrew, if you can trace your ancestry back to Abraham, you will be my special possession among all the nations." Rather, God said: "Now if you obey me fully and keep my covenant, then out of all nations you will be my treasured possession" (Exodus 19:5). John the Baptist put it this way: "Do not begin to say to yourselves, 'We have Abraham as our father.' For I tell you that out of these stones God can raise up children for Abraham" (Luke 3:8). It was a call to renew their identity as God's *laos*. It is not Abraham's blood that qualifies one for membership in the people of God; it is Abraham's faith!

Throughout OT history, Israel was often tempted to confuse its ethnic identity with its faith status. They had to be told repeatedly that it is not enough to be Jewish. Christians have also had a hard time learning this lesson. Over and over again, people have imagined that living in a so-called Christian land and attending (or even being members of) an official church somehow makes one truly Christian. This has never been the case.

The whole world belongs to God. Everyone belongs to God, the creator and sustainer of the whole world. But only those who confess the God of Israel, the Father of our Lord Jesus Christ, only those committed to a covenant relationship, and thus to membership in God's faith community, truly belong to the *laos* of God. Jewish roots (then) and Christian roots (now) simply don't count. Nor does political or cultural identification with Israel (then) or with a so-called Christian nation (now).

Nations cannot be Christian nations. Nations can only be the context where God's covenant people live, and where they seek to pledge their highest allegiance not to country and culture, but to God and their fellow covenant partners.

We can now begin to see more clearly that this was not an NT innovation in God's plan. It was not something John the Baptist or Jesus first introduced, not something that Pentecost finally solidified, not something that developed out of the missionary work of the early apostles. God had always intended to work this way. Within the national and cultural context of Israel, God was building a covenant community beyond national Israel. When we see that, we can also see how the church is God's intended continuation of Israel—that is, of *covenant* Israel, not of *ethnic* Israel.

## ONE COVENANT PEOPLE

If all of this gives the impression that God has two covenant peoples, the first one called Israel and the second called the church, then I have not been clear enough. On the contrary, the church is the *continuation* of OT Israel. What exactly this means, why it is so important, and what alternatives people have sometimes argued for will occupy us in the rest of this chapter.

The future of OT Israel is not the topic to be addressed here. Christians are significantly divided in their views concerning the status of contemporary Israel and its future. Does God guarantee them ultimate possession of the land of Israel?

Do the Scriptures guarantee that those Jews who, when Jesus returns, do not yet believe in him will have a second opportunity to come to faith, and that they will in fact do so? When we take biblical references to Israel and apply them in our world, do we connect them to ethnic Israel? To political Israel? To Israel as a faith community? Which of these, if any, will yet be special objects of God's redemptive work?

One reason Bible interpreters answer such questions so diversely is that a much more fundamental question is often insufficiently explored. That is this question: What happened in salvation history when God's people were reshaped by Jesus, by the coming of the Spirit at Pentecost, and by developments in the early church? Before that reshaping, the covenant people of God were understood to be a faith community closely tied to an ethnically Jewish community. After the reshaping, the covenant people of God were understood to be a multiethnic community of Jesus followers, growing out of Jewish roots but incorporating (without making them Jewish!) people of many tribes and nations. How did the reshaping happen, and what did it mean?

Two viewpoints are widely represented among Bible interpreters. It is important to understand both of these and how fundamentally different they are. This is particularly so because, in the end, I, along with a growing number of NT interpreters, endorse *neither* of them, but rather a quite different third option.

### Supersessionism and dispensationalism

Some interpreters of Scripture would claim this: Throughout OT history, God had only one covenant people, the people of Israel. But when God sent the Messiah Jesus, Israel did not accept Jesus as the coming Savior, so God elected a new people of God, the Gentile (non-Jewish) church of Jesus Christ. Israel had squandered its status as God's elect people. And so Israel is superseded by the church. The church inherits the promises first made to Israel. The literal, physical promises to Israel now find spiritual fulfillment in the church. This view has often been called supersessionism, and it has often resulted in anti-Semitism (and thus has also contributed to its most horrific expression, the Holocaust).

An alternative view is that the church does not *displace* Israel; the church is a *second* people of God *alongside* Israel. God first elected a national ethnic people, the people of Israel. When, in the course of salvation history, Israel rejected the Messiah, God *temporarily* set Israel aside. God brought into being a new people of God, the Christian church gathered around Jesus. But God never has and never will reject Israel. All God's promises to Israel will one day be fulfilled, and Israel will never cease to be the elect people of God. Many who hold this viewpoint develop it further. When Jesus comes and the church is raptured (taken to heaven), God will again establish Israel, lead Israel, and cause Israel to play a leading role among the nations of the earth. All the variations on this perspective are known as dispensationalism. In my view, an unfortunate consequence is that Christians uncritically support whatever is in the best interests of ethnic Jews in the nation-state of Israel, no matter what the consequences might be for Palestinians or other people groups.

Those who hold to supersessionism seem to accept that God jettisoned God's first plan for world redemption in favor of another. God went to plan B because humans were not prepared to support God in carrying out plan A. Given verses like Romans 3:3–4 and 11:29, it is hard to see how this view can be correct. Those who hold to dispensationalism (at least in its traditional form), whether they admit it or not, imply that a very large part of the Bible does not really apply to the Christian church. It is intended for Israel, not for us. That seems quite contrary to what the writers of the New Testament believed and practiced.

### The continuation alternative

A third possibility is gaining more and more acceptance by a wide range of leading biblical scholars (Krister Stendahl, E. P. Sanders, James D. G. Dunn, N. T. Wright, J. E. Toews, Luke T. Johnson, Richard B. Hays, and others). This view is that *the church is God's intended continuation of Israel.*

God has only one plan for the salvation of humanity. It began in the Old Testament and will continue until it is fulfilled. God's plan for Israel and God's plan for the church are the same because the church is God's intended continuation of what God began with Abraham. As theologian Gerhard Lohfink argues persuasively in *Jesus and Community*, Jesus did not come to found the church. He couldn't, for the church had been founded many centuries before Jesus came, when God brought into existence the covenant people of Israel. The church *is* God's Israel (see Galatians 6:16), the present form of God's renewed humanity. Jesus is the centerpiece of God's plan, the fulfillment of all that precedes his coming and the one who accomplishes all that God purposes for Israel and the church.

The introduction of a new term, *church*, instead of continuing with the first term, *Israel*, acknowledges that with Jesus' coming, God's plan for Israel took a giant leap forward. Jesus gathered those in Israel who were ready to move on with God's mission. He prepared them for the mission of incorporating into God's people others who had no Jewish heritage, ethnicity, or national identity. We sometimes refer to this as the "Gentile church," but for the first several decades of the Christian church it was almost entirely Jewish. Then through the rest of the first century (when the New Testament was being written), it remained a church strongly influenced by its Jewish roots, for its membership and its self-understanding were still quite Jewish.

Some interpret Paul's image of the olive tree in Romans 11:17–24 as if it separates between the Jewish people of God and the church. But that is precisely what it does *not* do.[1] No Gentile olive tree ever replaces a Jewish one. Nor does a Gentile olive tree stand alongside a Jewish one. Although defenders of supersessionism and dispensationalism often claim that their view is supported by the olive tree image, they seem to misread it. Both systems, in two different ways, reject the very image that Paul uses for God's people. There is and there can be only one olive tree. Branches can be broken off; branches can be grafted in. But the tree cannot be replaced or supplemented.

Some ask what happened to Israel when Israel "rejected" Jesus. The question is based on a false assumption. Israel did not reject Jesus! There is therefore no reason why Israel needed either to be replaced or to be supplemented. On the contrary, Israel was *divided* in its response to Jesus. When the gospel message spread to the Gentiles, the Gentile world was also divided in its response to Jesus. Believing Jews and believing Gentiles formed one body of Christ; thus we should not speak of a Gentile church.

The book of Acts first describes the early Jewish church, then narrates the stages that led this church to become a mixed Jew-Gentile church. What the church learned along the way was that Gentile believers did not need to become naturalized Jews to join the people of God.

We could say that another way: One can become a full member of God's Israel without becoming either ethnically or nationally Jewish. The church in Acts eventually learned that lesson, one that had already been taught, but not always caught, throughout OT history: True Israel is neither an ethnic nor a national people. True Israel is a covenant people. True Israel is a community of faith, a people living in covenant with God.

That does not mean that nothing changed with the coming of Jesus and with the coming of the Spirit at Pentecost. God's plan was for Israel to be blessed to be a blessing, to know God to make God known, to experience God's goodness to draw others into that same experience of God's grace. But the assumption throughout the Old Testament was that God's grace and goodness and presence and voice would be experienced and heard *in Israel*. Others would find God *among the Israelites*.

In the book of Acts we see that the early (Jewish!) Christians were led to take the next step: to scatter among the Gentiles and from the original Jewish core to grow into a multiethnic community that gave Jewish ethnicity no priority over any other ethnicity, Jewish nationality no priority over any other nationality. The church learned to distinguish between two concepts that had often been confused with each other: the concepts of *ethnic* identity and of *covenant* identity—that is, the concepts of *ethnos* and of *laos*.

Israel, *as a faith community*, was renewed with the coming of Jesus, was empowered and recommissioned with the coming of the Spirit, was recognized and authorized as a multiethnic covenant people with the Jerusalem Council, and was separated from certain aspects of its Jewish cultural and national heritage with the destruction of Israel as a nation in 70 AD.

Throughout history, the church has faced the same temptation that ancient Israel faced, the temptation to confuse national identity with faith identity. Israel acquired land, sometimes justified and sometimes unjustified; Israel became a powerful nation-state, sometimes following God's direction and sometimes resisting it; and Israel did many more things that are typical behaviors for ethnic and political bodies. Israel's big mistake was thinking that this was a covenant community expressing its identity. It was not. It was an ethnic national entity expressing its identity. To be a faithful covenant people was something else altogether.

As full participants in the people of God, Christians not of Jewish ethnic origin ought to be eternally grateful for those in Israel who recognized their true calling and who, commissioned by Jesus and empowered by the Spirit, moved beyond Israel's ethnic boundaries to include Gentile believers. When our highest allegiance is to ethnicity or nation—worse still, when we think that our ethnicity and nation is the very definition of covenant faithfulness—then we need to hear the prophetic call to repent, just as Israel did.

## THE IMPORTANCE OF CONTINUATION

I have belabored this point because when we grasp it, we are outfitted with a new set of glasses that shape how we read the entire Bible. Then we understand the main point of Stephen's sermon in Acts 7. The part of Israel that was ready to recognize Jesus as Messiah inherited Israel's faith history. Those people are the true Israel, and we have now joined them.

Then we also understand what really happened at the Jerusalem Council (Acts 15). Here the leaders of the church, virtually all of them still Jewish, discerned a way to keep the church from dividing along ethnic lines. By incorporating

Gentiles into the body of Christ they clarified the basis of their own salvation. "He did not discriminate between us and them, for he purified their hearts by faith. . . . We believe it is through the grace of our Lord Jesus that we are saved, just as they are." (Acts 15:9, 11).

Nobody is saved by belonging to a particular ethnic group. All are saved by the grace of God. Therefore, Gentiles are joined to the people of God *as Gentiles*. And that is how "David's fallen tent" is rebuilt (Acts 15:16).

I have already alluded to the olive tree image in Romans 11. Branches are broken off; new ones are grafted in. They represent people, both Jewish and Gentile, who through faith are incorporated into, and who through unbelief are removed from, the one people of God. Ancestral origin and ethnic identity neither exclude nor guarantee inclusion. Only through faith can anyone belong to the one true (and now ethnically mixed) people of God.

Now we come to the most important implication of all this. *The whole Bible is God's word addressed to us!* As NT Christians, if we do not recognize that we belong to the same faith community as Abraham, Moses, David, and Esther, then we would find little in the Old Testament to apply to ourselves. If we draw a sharp dividing line between the Old Testament (supposedly addressed to Israel) and the New Testament (the part addressed to NT Christians), we declare three-quarters of the Bible to be virtually irrelevant for readers like us.

But it gets worse. If we separate out in Scripture all the content seemingly directed toward the Jews and only pay attention to what was directed toward what we call "the Gentile church," we will also lose well over half the New Testament. Most prominently, we will lose the Gospels, for they record the life, ministry, and teaching of Jesus among his ethnic and national compatriots, the Jews. If we make Pentecost the point where God's messengers finally begin to address us, the church, then we will have a very small Bible indeed.

No, God's entire written Word, from Genesis through Revelation, is directed toward God's covenant community. Earlier parts addressed that covenant community while it was still embedded within (but never identical with) an ethnic people. Later parts addressed that covenant community after it had been sent forth into all the world to gather believers from all nations. It was always designed to speak to the whole people of God, and thus it speaks now to all Christians, in all times and places. From Genesis through Revelation, the Bible addresses us.

This covenant people is still on that journey begun so long ago with the call of Abraham. We have not yet reached that point where "the full number of the Gentiles has come in, and in this way all Israel will be saved" (Romans 11:25–26), but we are well on the way to that goal. We can already sing, along with the saints of all ages:

> You [Jesus] are worthy to take the scroll
>     and to open its seals,
> because you were slain,
>     and with your blood you purchased for God
>     persons from every tribe and language and people and nation.
> You have made them to be a kingdom and priests to serve our God,
>     and they will reign on the earth.
> (Revelation 5:9–10)

Precisely that which was promised to the people of Israel, "You will be for me a kingdom of priests and a holy nation"

(Exodus 19:6), now finds its fulfillment in the church of Jesus
Christ. We who belong to that church have not replaced Israel.
Nor have we become a second people of God beside them. We
have joined them. And we now have the privilege of fulfilling
the destiny for which *they* (that is, *we*) were called into existence in the first place.

## WHAT DO WE LEARN FROM STUDYING THE NATURE OF THE PEOPLE OF GOD?

These considerations about the one people of God are crucial
for understanding how the Old Testament speaks to us. The
history of Israel is *our* story. Once *we* were not a people, but
God called *our* father Abraham and formed of his descendants
a people group as numerous as the stars of the sky and the
sand on the seashore. Once *we* were enslaved in Egypt, but
God delivered *us*. God gathered *us* at the foot of Mount Sinai
and made a covenant with *us*. God promised to be *our* faithful
covenant partner and called *us* to be faithful covenant partners with God in response.

From our NT perspective, we can continue the narrative.
God came down to live among *us* in the person of God's very
own Son, Jesus. Through Jesus' life, ministry, teaching, death,
and resurrection, God continued to bring *us* closer and closer
to that destiny for which *we* exist. God then empowered *us*
with the Holy Spirit and sent *us* into all the world to preach
the good news. We rejoice in what God has already done, but
we also long for the day when Jesus will come again and bring
God's great salvation project to completion.

# Questions for discussion

1. "True Israel is neither an ethnic nor a national people. True Israel is a covenant people. True Israel is a community of faith, a people living in covenant with God. . . . The church is God's intended continuation of Israel." These are the central points of this chapter. How do you respond to the arguments put forward in defense of these viewpoints? What are the implications of all this?

2. "To be ethnically Jewish and to be a member of God's covenant people group are never identical concepts, no matter how much or how little overlap there is between those who are the one and those who are the other." The mistakes that Israel sometimes made in this regard have been and still are also perpetuated by Christians. Sometimes we invest more significance in our ethnic or national identity than in our identity as the people of God. Do you agree with these observations? Where do you see evidence of this in your context?

3. "God gathered *us* at the foot of Mount Sinai and made a covenant with *us*. God promised to be *our* faithful covenant partner and called *us* to be faithful covenant partners with God in response." If we were really convinced of this, how would that affect the way we view the Old Testament and the people group whose story is narrated there?

# GOD'S CHILDREN FROM BIRTH TO ADULTHOOD

*Come to me, all you who are weary and burdened, and I will give you rest.* —Matthew 11:28

*Let anyone who is thirsty come to me and drink.* —John 7:37

*There is rejoicing in the presence of the angels of God over one sinner who repents.* —Luke 15:10

Jesus came to seek and find, to invite and welcome, to bring home those who had gone astray. Jesus was doing exactly what Yahweh God had always done for a wayward people. Indeed, the story of humanity, of Israel of old, and of the church today, is so often a story of God's unending search to find and bring home those who have wandered away.

The main storyline of the Old Testament is not the story of Israel. Rather, it is the story of God and God's unrelenting grace. Despite all human failure, God is a faithful God who invites and welcomes, receives and restores.

❖

The Old Testament does not aim to provide an objective history of Israel. The goal is to reveal God at work. The first six chapters of this book examined the first seventy chapters in the Old Testament (less than 10 percent of the total text). We need to cover the remaining chapters of the Old Testament more quickly, so I present to you the history of Israel in under two hundred words.

> To reach all nations, God created Israel out of Abraham and his descendants. In Egypt, God protected them from starvation. In the exodus, God rescued them from Egyptian slavery. At Mount Sinai, God established a covenant of loyalty with Israel, then led and protected them through forty years of desert wandering. God then led them into the promised land, where they conquered enemies and lived among foreigners. There God's people were to serve God with their whole hearts and establish an alternative society, where justice and equality would be preserved and modeled among the nations. At first Israel was led by judges, with prophets and priests mediating God's word and God's forgiveness. Then came the monarchy, reluctantly permitted by God. After three kings the nation split into two nations. The northern ten tribes fell from covenant faithfulness and were taken captive by the Syrians. Most never returned. The southern two tribes were eventually taken into Babylonian captivity, a punishment for their unfaithfulness. After power shifted to the Persians, God permitted Israel to return. Nehemiah and Ezra led renewal movements, and many returned to faithfulness as they longed for a promised redeemer to restore Israel.

This brief summary supplies the grid into which we fit all the parts of God's larger story. We find in the Old Testament a set of portraits and glimpses of God's interactions with the chosen people and the rest of the world, told from many different perspectives. This chapter explores some of those perspectives, starting with a graphic text from the Prophets.

## ISRAEL THE SON; ISRAEL THE OX

When Israel was a child, I loved him,
> and out of Egypt I called my son.

But the more they were called,
> the more they went away from me.

They sacrificed to the Baals
> and they burned incense to images.

It was I who taught Ephraim to walk,
> taking them by the arms;

but they did not realize
> it was I who healed them.

I led them with cords of human kindness,
> with ties of love.

To them I was like one who lifts
> a little child to the cheek,
> and I bent down to feed them.

(Hosea 11:1–4 TNIV)

Various images of God flow in and out of each other in these four verses, no matter how the text is interpreted and translated. Interpreters do not all agree with the way it is translated above. In some renditions the imagery changes in the last two verses. The Hebrew words can be read so that the image shifts from a parent training up a child to a farmer caring tenderly for an ox (the most common beast of burden for ancient Israel). Here are these verses in the New Living Translation: "I led Israel along with my ropes of kindness and love. I lifted the yoke from his neck, and I myself stooped to feed him." I favor this reading while still recognizing that the dominant metaphor comes from parenting.

Let's begin with that metaphor. While the text does not indicate whether a father or a mother is being depicted, the first readers probably would have assumed the latter because of the assumed role differentiation in their world. Fathers are just as capable as mothers of teaching infants to walk, of taking young children in their arms, and so on, but the first readers likely would have seen this as a portrait of God playing the role of a gentle and nurturing mother.

And then, according to some translations, the image switches to a farmer, highlighting the masculine role. This farmer lightens the load of the ox (an interesting role reversal!) and even bends down to feed the ox. In the English language the idea of an ox might conjure ideas of stubbornness, or perhaps inflexibility. In those days, however, the ox was an important family helper, a valued contributor to the family's well-being. Jesus once asked, "If one of you has a child or an ox that falls into a well on the Sabbath day, will you not immediately pull it out?" (Luke 14:5). Jesus did not intend to put children and oxen on the same level, but he did reveal the tender care that people would guarantee both children and household animals. Consider also Deuteronomy 25:4, where God commands, "Do not muzzle an ox while it is treading out the grain," and the NT interpretation of this as support for the claim: "The worker deserves his wages" (1 Timothy 5:18). Indeed, the ox was a beloved animal. Yet the main picture in the Hosea 11 text is that of an even more dearly loved child.

What is the prophet saying about God with these images? First, God brought Israel to birth, into God's own family, as a dear son. As "God's son," Israel bears God's image. God not only brings Israel to life; God also nourishes and trains and leads Israel, the son, to maturity. But when Israel, the son in this family, is old enough to make his own decisions, he runs away from God. In youthful rebellion, Israel runs after other gods. The covenant of faithfulness that is supposed to bind Israel to God is strained, stretched, and finally ignored. God has done everything possible for Israel, the son. With motherly love, God has taught Israel how to walk, has taken Israel in arm. As a gentle, caring farmer, God has lightened Israel's load, has stooped to meet Israel's every need. Israel, in response, has ignored God's compassion and care, taken no notice that God has done everything possible to care for and train Israel. Israel has simply abandoned all that, run after other gods, and ignored God's invitation to return.

God responds by leading Israel gently back home, if only Israel will come. One translation of verse 4 says of God, "I drew them to me" (GNT); another, "I led them with kindness and with love, not with ropes" (CEV). Why did God need to entice Israel to come back? God brought Israel into existence, rescued Israel from Egypt, made a covenant of loyalty with Israel, cared for Israel, did for Israel what Israel could not have done for itself. Israel belongs fully to God. But Israel has run away. And now God tries to *win* Israel back? Why not just *take* Israel back? Because God respects Israel's free choices, whether they are for or against God. With love and patience, God calls and waits and hopes that Israel will freely choose to come back.

That is really the OT story—God provides for Israel; Israel runs away; God never gives up hope of winning Israel back to faithfulness. These three aspects of the OT story deserve closer scrutiny.

## GOD'S PROVISION FOR ISRAEL

In the wilderness, God provided manna and quail for Israel (Exodus 16:4–15), and in the promised land, milk and honey (Numbers 13:27). Whether Israel received these provisions through miraculous interventions or through what we call the normal course of nature, God was the provider. The promised land itself was an expression of God's provision. There Israel had room to spread out and grow, and more importantly, to live out its mission as a light on the hill, showing all the world how God blesses a people living in covenant relationship with God.

On its own Israel could never become the model society God intended Israel to be. So God gave concrete instructions for their economic and interpersonal relationships. These also represented God's gracious provision. There was the tithe, designed to pay for important aspects of their religious life and to support those in need "so that the Levites (who have no allotment or inheritance of their own) and the foreigners, the fatherless and the widows who live in your towns may come and eat and be satisfied, and so that the LORD your God may bless you in all the work of your hands" (Deuteronomy 14:29).

Loans were to be given generously and with no interest charged so that the rich would not profit from the poverty of others (Leviticus 25:36). The Sabbath was held so that worship of God and fellowship among God's people could be given proper priority, so that they could concretely express trust in God and not their own labor as the ultimate provider, and so that neither servants nor animals were overburdened. The Sabbath was to be a holy day, set apart to honor God, the creator, the emancipator, and the provider.

The Sabbath year was a whole year of sabbath rest for people and land (see Leviticus 25:4–5). It also leveled out social and economic inequities. Loans were commuted into gifts; slaves were set free.

Then there was the most radical of all the divine provisions: the Jubilee Year. Leviticus 25 indicates that every fifty years, not only were debts to be cancelled and enslaved people freed, but land was to revert to the original landowners, reproducing the original equality that God intended. Some of these don't sound much like provisions to us. They sound like unjust economic requirements. But that reveals how out of step our modern ideas of justice are with God's. Many of us imagine that we are the owners of the land we call ours. God made sure Israel never reached this conclusion: "The land must not be sold permanently, because the land is mine and you reside in my land as foreigners and strangers" (Leviticus 25:23).

Did Israel really practice all these instructions? Certainly not always, or we would not hear the recurring word of the prophets: "'Bring the whole tithe into the storehouse, that there may be food in my house. Test me in this,' says the LORD Almighty, 'and see if I will not throw open the floodgates of heaven and pour out so much blessing that there will not be room enough to store it'" (Malachi 3:10). Israel did not understand that all these instructions were designed for their benefit. How blessed they would have been if they had practiced the Jubilee! Unfortunately, there is no evidence that they ever did. They simply did not trust God enough to believe God was doing it all for their own benefit. Are things much different today?

God also shows Israel how to get along with their neighbors. We sometimes think that "loving our enemies" is something novel that Jesus instituted in the New Testament. But God told Israel, even before they entered the promised land: "When a foreigner resides among you in your land, do not mistreat them. The foreigner residing among you must be treated as your native-born. Love them as yourself, for you were foreigners in Egypt. I am the LORD your God" (Leviticus 19:33–34). If Israel had truly practiced that, what a city on the hill, what a light in the darkness Israel would have been! When they failed to be that, the missing element was never God's care and provision; it was always Israel's unwillingness to live by God's radical instructions.

God also provided for Israel through godly leadership. Again, from Israel's side, it didn't always turn out as intended. Too often, godly leaders departed from their earlier faithfulness. Still, when Israel was led astray, God kept sending servants to invite them back: judges like Deborah and Gideon; kings like David and Josiah; prophets like Samuel and Elijah; reformers like Ezra and Nehemiah. That doesn't mean that these servants were completely faithful. Gideon led Israel into false worship; David committed adultery and murder. Yet despite human leaders like this, God provided leadership for Israel, helping them "grow up" as God's "son."

In truth, God's acts of discipline and punishment should also be counted as divine provision. When Israel didn't understand any other language, God pronounced judgment on Israel so that through discipline God might bring them back onto the right path. Sometimes God used natural disasters, sometimes foreign armies, sometimes world powers that took Israel into captivity. Each of these was designed to help lead Israel to maturity. Sometimes these measures had their intended effect, sometimes they did not.

## ISRAEL RUNS AWAY

We read in Hosea 11:1–4 how God's people responded to their gentle, caring parent. Like an ungrateful child, Israel ran away from it all. There were always individual exceptions, faithful people who aimed to remain true to God (such as Elijah; 1 Kings 19:4, 18). And there were times of national revival when Israel turned back to God, repented, changed their ways, and worshiped God sincerely. Yet so often we see Israel playing the role of an ungrateful child running away from a loving parent. Sometimes the prophets changed the image to an unfaithful wife, committing adultery with foreign gods. "You adulterous wife! You prefer strangers to your own husband!" (Ezekiel 16:32).

Let's recall the three great promises that God gave Israel when they made a covenant with each other at Mount Sinai:

1. I will provide for you.
2. I will fight for you.
3. I will lead you.

It was precisely in these three respects that Israel failed God. Instead of trusting God to keep these promises, they either sought these things from other gods or, just as often, relied on their own human resources to take care of these concerns.

Because God had promised *to provide for Israel*, Israel ought to have been a generous people. Since God had promised to meet all their needs, there should have been no hesitation in bringing in the full tithe. If they had been generous with those in need, a society would have been created where everyone's needs were met. Instead, Israel frequently refused to bring in the tithes, to care for the needy, and to trust God. They bowed down to other gods, trusting in fertility gods like Baal and Asherah to guarantee abundance. They thought their pagan worship (often involving sexual practice) would produce earthly fertility. God abhorred and condemned these practices, not only because they were a misuse of sexuality, but because they represented idolatrous unfaithfulness.

Israel was not always ready to trust God *to fight for Israel*. Later chapters will consider the problem of war in the Old Testament. Here, let it suffice to say that Israel was supposed to place trust in God, not in military machinery and foreign treaties. God's word to Israel was: "The LORD will fight for you; you need only to be still" (Exodus 14:14). They were not supposed to assemble the largest army in the Middle East. In this area as well, Israel was unfaithful. They even based their demand for a king on the supposed necessity of military strength: "We want a king over us. Then we will be like all the other nations, with a king to lead us and to go out before us and fight our battles'" (1 Samuel 8:19–20). Israel's demand was a rejection of God as protector.

Israel was not willing for God *to lead Israel*. Or at least they wanted God to lead them through a human king. Why? That was how other nations set things up. Israel clamored for the same arrangement. They wanted to be "like all the other nations"! But God had intended things to be different in Israel. God wanted to be Israel's king. God wanted to personally lead this special called-out people. There would naturally be various human leaders as well. Judges would seek to understand God's righteous judgments and bring them to bear in concrete situations. Prophets would listen for God's voice and speak it forth to the people. Priests had the task of mediating both human worship of God and God's forgiveness of the people.

When Israel demanded a king, they were departing from God's intended leadership structure. As soon as Israel instituted the monarchy, the kings (and occasionally queens) became the real powerbrokers, and other religious leaders were at their mercy. At times things deteriorated to the point that Israel really did abandon God. Only God's covenant faithfulness and mercy bound God to Israel in those times.

God was a God who faithfully provided; Israel responded unfaithfully. God responded by remaining faithful and working to restore Israel to faithfulness.

## GOD WINS ISRAEL BACK

From the start of Israel's covenant relationship with God, God had instructed Israel on the importance and the nature of worship. Central to this worship was the tabernacle that Israel was to construct. Significantly, the tabernacle was a tent, something that could be repeatedly taken down and set up. This symbolized that God was traveling with Israel, a faithful companion on the equally symbolic journey from slavery in Egypt to rest in the promised land (2 Samuel 7:6). God led Israel from the front (a pillar of cloud and pillar of fire signaled that it was time to move; Exodus 13:21) and lived in their midst (the cloud covered the tabernacle when they camped; Numbers 9:18). Thus the tabernacle symbolized and made possible God's presence amid the covenant people, whether they camped or moved on.

This deepens the picture language that the author of John uses to describe the coming of Jesus: "The Word became flesh and made his dwelling [set up tent] among us. We have seen his glory" (John 1:14). And it heightens the vision of God's presence finally "tenting" among humanity at the end of this age. "Look! God's dwelling place [tent] is now among the people, and he will dwell with them. They will be his people, and God himself will be with them and be their God" (Revelation 21:3).

In the Old Testament, the tabernacle is called the tent of meeting. There, Israel gathered and worshiped God, sought God's forgiveness, reminded themselves of God's past and present provision, and renewed the covenant. Israel was not a holy people merely *when they gathered at the meeting place.*

Rather, at the tent of meeting they gained clarity and help so they could live as a holy people, a people set apart for God's purposes, *in all of life*. Christian gatherings ought to accomplish similar functions. As we gather in God's presence, we discover together what it means to live as a covenant people in all of life, and we gain the resources we need to put this into practice. So we continue to return to God, in worship and in daily living.

The system of offerings was designed to enable the "runaway child" to come back home. When God's people forgot who their provider was, they were reminded through the thank offering to give God the glory for all they had. When their sins blocked God's intimate presence, offerings for forgiveness and cleansing restored the relationship. Individual worshipers did not presume to step into God's immediate presence; indeed, they could not. The consecrated priests mediated God's presence for them. And so God repeatedly welcomed the wayward children back home, back into God's presence, and the covenant was renewed.

Later, the temple assumed the role of the tabernacle. Whereas God was the one who commanded the construction of the tent, the temple was more a human desire, another way in which Israel wanted to be "like all the other nations" (as with the monarchy). Yet God used the temple to live among the people and be the focus of their worship and their fellowship.

At times, Israel seemed to focus more on the temple than on God's presence there, relying on the ceremonies themselves for their status with God and their security as God's people. Yet God insisted that what really mattered was the sincerity of the heart and the faithful life. "For I desire mercy, not sacrifice, and acknowledgment of God rather than burnt offerings" (Hosea 6:6). Much later, Jesus affirmed the religious leader who correctly said, "God is one and there is no other but him. To love him with all your heart, with all your understanding and with all your strength, and to love your neighbor as yourself is more important than all burnt offerings and sacrifices" (Mark 12:32–33).

God's attempts to win Israel back were often carried out through the prophets, spokespersons for God, interpreting God's ways, calling for repentance, assuring God's people that if they returned, they would be forgiven. At times God worked through special leaders, like the priest and teacher Ezra and the state official Nehemiah, renewing Israel in covenant faithfulness.

Not to be overlooked is the role of the law (torah) in winning back the wayward child. Here we should think not so much of the five books of the Law, but of the content of God's covenant itself. When Israel understood the law's true function and allowed themselves to be guided by God's torah, they discovered what a gift it was. "Let your compassion come to me that I may live, for your law is my delight" (Psalm 119:77). "Great peace have those who love your law, and nothing can make them stumble" (119:165).

And then there were the written Scriptures. Book by book, the collection grew as Israel heard from God and reflected on God's ways. Sometimes the written texts themselves led Israel back to God. In Josiah's day, for example, because the Scriptures had been forgotten, Israel had wandered away from God, and when these same Scriptures were rediscovered, Israel was led back (see 2 Kings 23).

We do not read of synagogues within the Old Testament. They developed during the last centuries of the OT period. They were prayer houses, schoolhouses, and houses of worship. Synagogues were forerunners of Christian gathering places: locations to hear God's word, experience fellowship, worship God, and deliberate together what it means to be God's covenant people.

Finally, we must mention prophetic promises. God called Israel back to faithfulness through promises that kept hope alive. In dark times, God would speak through the prophets: "See, I am doing a new thing! Now it springs up; do you not perceive it? I am making a way in the wilderness and streams in the wasteland" (Isaiah 43:19). Israel was invited to join God on a journey leading to the fulfillment of all God's purposes.

The Old Testament ends with many prophecies still unfulfilled. Israel was challenged to trust that God would be a faithful covenant partner whose word cannot fail. And it did not! One day, God's chosen servant, representing God's very presence on earth, announced: "The time has come. . . . The kingdom of God has come near. Repent and believe the good news!" (Mark 1:15).

If everything in the Old Testament were so encouraging and full of hope, the next two chapters of this book would not be necessary. Yet Bible readers often stumble over a host of OT texts and themes that can be difficult to understand or accept. Instead of pretending these don't exist, we will take a closer look at some of these and try to find our way through.

## WHAT CAN WE LEARN FROM STUDYING GOD'S PEOPLE FROM BIRTH TO ADULTHOOD?

One author, after highlighting a host of "problems" with the Old Testament, claims the following: "But the above issues are of lesser significance compared to another problem, one that pervades the whole of the Old Testament: it is dark. From beginning to end it is a story of self-destructive evil. . . . The story of Israel is one of almost unmitigated failure."[1]

I could not disagree more! The story of Israel contains a great deal of failure. But the main storyline of the Old Testament is not the story *of Israel*. It is the story *of God*. Far from being a "dark story," it is a story of unrelenting grace. Despite all human failure, God is a faithful God who invites and welcomes, receives and restores.

What was true for Israel is true for the church today, indeed for all humanity. That is why studying Israel's story is so very relevant for us as well.

## *Questions for discussion*

1.  Provision—running away—winning back! Do you agree that the main storyline of Israel's history can be summed up in these three movements? Where else in Scripture to you see this pattern recurring—for Israel, for the church, for individuals?

2.  What relevance do you see for the people of God today in OT mandates like the Sabbath (a day of rest each week), the Sabbath year (debt forgiveness and release of enslaved people every seventh year), and the Jubilee (liberty for all and redistribution of land every fiftieth year)?

3.  What significance do you see for the church today in OT institutions and provisions like the tabernacle, the temple, the system of offerings, the law, and prophetic promises?

# PROBLEMATIC PORTRAITS OF GOD, PUNISHMENT, AND MIRACLE REPORTS

*If you really know me, you will know my Father as well. . . .
Anyone who has seen me has seen the Father. —John 14:7, 9*

The point of the John 14 text is a lot more radical than we might suppose. It is not merely another proof text verifying our confessional claim that Jesus is God. Jesus is saying, "If you want to know what the Father is like, just look at me. I am here to show you." The best way to glimpse what God is really like is to observe carefully what Jesus is like. Jesus reveals the heart of God in his person, attitudes, priorities, and way of relating to people.

If we are troubled by some of the OT portraits of God or other aspects of the Old Testament, we are invited to look to Jesus, who both affirms and supplements what God had previously revealed to God's people.

❖

I have heard people describe their experience with the Old Testament something like this: "I started reading it. It was interesting for a while. And then somewhere along the way I just lost interest. Sometimes it was boring, sometimes incomprehensible. It made claims I just couldn't believe. And I had a hard time figuring out what all this had to do with me anyway. I finally just gave up."

Such a pity! But I understand that point of view. During my childhood my father would read three chapters of scripture every morning while the oatmeal was getting cold. I owe much of my Bible knowledge to this, but I won't lie. My siblings and I often just tuned out while the reading went on and on and seemed neither interesting nor important. Today I find the Old Testament (mostly) fascinating. I think this is because I've learned a lot more about how language works and how stories work. I've also learned how to deal with some of the topics that sometimes seemed most troubling.

In this chapter and the next, I will share some perspectives on important, but sometimes head-scratching, issues that arise when we encounter OT scripture. My hope is that some of these reflections will connect with the concerns of readers who also struggle to value the Old Testament and receive it as God's Word.

## PORTRAITS OF THE ONE TRUE GOD

One day we will see God "face to face" (1 Corinthians 13:12). Until then, we have only human words to describe God. And that is precisely the problem. Words cannot really grasp the nature of God very well. And that is no less true when we find these words in the Bible than when we use them to write our creeds and theology books. These words aim to convey something language cannot capture.

There are some systematic theology books out there that I truly appreciate. But some that I encountered as a young Bible student set me off in the wrong direction altogether. I remember one that had a long list of abstract "attributes" of God: omnipotence, omniscience, omnipresence, immutability, impassibility, aseity (and quite a few more "omnis" and "ities"). If I am not mistaken it listed eighteen attributes. For each, the author supplied about five Bible texts (usually taken out of context) "proving" that God really had each of these attributes.

As we studied this book and "verified" each "proof text," we proudly concluded we had God all figured out. (By the way, I just checked Wikipedia and discovered that God has gained nine new attributes since that book was written.[1])

At some point I began to wonder if anyone could understand *me* by listing *my* eighteen (or twenty-seven) attributes and collecting evidence that each one truly applied to me. I have become rather skeptical that we can learn much about God by generating and defending attributes and thus creating doctrines about God.

Instead of abstract doctrines about God, the Old Testament offers us graphic and inspiring portraits of God that help us discern the roles that God plays (creator, king, shepherd, and so on). If we want to understand God better, we benefit more from these than from lists of doctrines. Admittedly, this alternative approach is not without challenges:

- First, we can hardly deny that alongside the "beautiful portraits" are others that leave us scratching our heads. Does God really wake up from a sound sleep "as a warrior wakes from the stupor of wine" (Psalm 78:65)? Does God really place bets with Satan (Job 2:3–6)? Does God deliberately go and deceive prophets (1 Kings 22:22)?

- Second, even when we examine the more "acceptable" portraits, we don't always know which aspect of the portrait (or which feature of the metaphor) is in focus. If God is a king, does that imply primarily majesty? Or monarchical rule? If God is a potter, does that make each of us subject to God's every whim? Or uniquely special? One way to avoid the challenge of discerning is to just write doctrines, but at what cost?

- Third, some consider it unworthy of the God of the universe to be described with commonplace images and human roles. Wouldn't abstract philosophical concepts seem more appropriate to a deity beyond human understanding? The problem is, the philosophical God we end up defining often looks much more like the deity Plato aimed to define than the one who walked with Adam and Eve in the garden and with David through the valley of the shadow of death. It's hard for me to imagine Jesus contemplating eighteen (or twenty-seven) attributes and naming the end result "Abba."

I think I understand why some Bible interpreters gravitate toward doctrines of God rather than to the images and portraits supplied in Scripture. But the cost of doing so is steep indeed.

By deemphasizing those images of God that we find difficult, we risk also losing the incredibly beautiful, comforting, motivating, challenging images on the other side. When we closely examine the various biblical portraits of God as creator, as shepherd, as vineyard owner, as potter (and dozens more), we are drawn into a deeper understanding of our place within God's creation, our calling, our source of meaning, and our security and comfort in hard times.

Alongside the developed portraits are also graphic metaphors and evocative titles for God: the Lord Who Heals (Jehovah Rapha); Lord God Almighty (El Shaddai); the Lord Who Provides (Jehovah Jireh); and many more. Focusing on portraits, images, and titles helps us learn to live in relationship with our God, even if it does not give us the false security of having God all figured out.

But there is another problem with the "attributes approach" to defining God. Those who practice it often cling to philosophical concepts for which they find some meager support in a few proof texts, but which substantially distort how God is presented in Scripture. It may well be that the mythical gods of the ancient Greeks could be ascribed qualities like simplicity, immutability, impassibility, but the God of the Bible? Simplicity—ascribed to the triune God, who is mysterious beyond understanding? Impassibility—ascribed to the God who suffers with us and for us? Immutability—ascribed to the God who becomes incarnate in Jesus of Nazareth and thus joins God with humanity for all eternity?

God's people were forbidden to create visual images of God (Exodus 20:4), but they were repeatedly inspired to paint word pictures. We are invited to catch glimpses of God through these portraits while guarding against imagining they are exact replicas. We don't try to wring as many points of comparison out of each image and metaphor as possible. They draw us into relationship with a beautiful, mysterious, ever-faithful God. If that does not seem fully satisfying, we remind ourselves that until we see God face-to-face, we will always see "like puzzling reflections in a mirror" (1 Corinthians 13:12 NLT). And so we guard against claiming more clarity than God has given us.

Moreover, it had always been God's plan that the clearest revelation of the divine nature would come neither through doctrinal claims nor through portraits and metaphors, but rather through the living, breathing, visible, approachable incarnation of God in the person of Jesus of Nazareth (Hebrews 1:1–3). And it remains God's plan to give even further clarity to who God is and what God is like not by enlightened theological reflection, but by showing up so that we can see God face-to-face (1 John 3:1).

The OT portraits of God are nevertheless an important part of God's self-revelation to humans and specifically to God's people. And they reveal God most helpfully when we take seriously the following points of view:

- The picture language of the Old Testament never intended to provide complete clarity about the nature of God. God reserved this for the first and second comings of Jesus.

- Most images of God use human traits that we know to be only partly true of God. God does not literally have body parts like hands and arms. When the Bible uses such language, we call this anthropomorphism. We should note that even traits like *merciful*, *faithful*, and *angry* employ anthropomorphism. These terms do not mean exactly the same things when referring to God as they do when describing people.

- The images of God reflect the perspective of the OT people of God. By this I do not mean they are *merely* human attempts to grasp God. The Old Testament would not really be God's Word if it contained no more than human perceptions. Indeed, the God of the Old Testament would in that case be little more than any other local ancient Near Eastern deity, described by a people group to reflect the private fears and aspirations of those who worshiped it. In the Old Testament, God is not only the one being portrayed, but the one supplying the portraits. That said, God's revelation came to God's people in a language and in terms they understood. The more we learn to read the Old Testament from the perspective of its authors and first readers, the more helpful we will find the images of God within its pages.

- Ultimately, the New Testament shows us more clearly than the Old Testament alone what God is like. God knew that the OT images were not enough. That is one of the reasons why God came in the flesh to be among us. We look at Jesus and we see God. The impressions we gain from the Old Testament alone are often corrected or completed by Jesus, by the words he spoke about God, and by the way his own life revealed God. With corrected perspectives, we can often revisit the Old Testament and see what may have been previously missed.

With these thoughts in mind, let's consider some of the most important ways that God is portrayed within the Old Testament.

### God as creator and sustainer

God created the heavens and the earth, and all their inhabitants. These are God's handiwork and reflect God's glory (Psalm 19:1). On this canvas a special role is given to humans and in particular to the people of God, brought into existence by God's divine intervention. Uniquely among all God's creatures, we can choose to live for God's glory or not to, and we can understand why doing so is appropriate to who God is and to whom God made us. God has preserved the universe in the face of destructive powers and continues to sustain planet Earth despite all the ways that humans exploit it and unwisely steward or abuse its resources. Creator God is also re-creator God. Already in the Old Testament, the promise of a renewed heaven and earth points the way toward creation's rebirth that began with Jesus' resurrection and will be completed at his return.

### God as savior

The salvation of the world and of humanity from the power of sin and its destructive effects is the main message of the whole Bible. In the last two chapters of the Bible (Revelation 21–22) we encounter a (future) saved world and a humanity that is finally ready to continue the story that the first two chapters of the Bible began. This will not be the end of all things, but a whole new beginning!

### God as covenant partner

In the Old Testament, God repeatedly drew humans into covenant partnership. In the New Testament, this covenant offer is made through Jesus to the renewed people of God (Luke 22:20). God is always faithful to these covenant partners, even when they fail. We are invited into intimate relationship with the God of the universe who cares for us, protects us, guides us, and ultimately shapes history along with us as it moves ever closer to its God-shaped destiny. What an incredible God!

### God as husband

The previous chapter examined the OT portrait of God as faithful parent. That is a central image of God in both Testaments. But in both Testaments, family imagery also goes beyond just that, especially in its presentation of God as a husband. It is therefore not surprising that God's revelation sometimes reflects a worldview that considers the husband the one responsible for the welfare of the entire family. "God as husband" is not primarily about gender. God is also represented in the Old Testament with traditionally feminine traits (e.g., Isaiah 66:12–13). This image of God as husband illustrates that the relationship between God and God's people is an intimate love relationship, one where God always remains faithful and always offers forgiveness and restored relationship, even when the "wife" (God's covenant partner) is unfaithful to God (Hosea 3:1).

### God as warrior

The covenant that God made with Israel clarified that Israel's national security would be God's responsibility. Israel was thus called to represent a radical alternative to the ways of the surrounding peoples, who relied on kings and their militaries for protection and conquest. Israel's alliances were to be with God alone, not with other nations, for God would be the one who would fight for Israel. "A horse is a vain hope for deliverance; despite all its great strength it cannot save. . . . We wait in hope for the LORD; he is our help and our shield" (Psalm 33:17, 20). "Unless the LORD watches over the city, the guards stand watch in vain" (127:1)

### God as king

Israel was called to be radically different from the neighboring peoples, and that included their form of government. Instead of a monarchy, Israel was to be led by godly, religious leaders (judges, prophets, and priests) under the sovereign rule of God. Israel, however, wanted a king. After many warnings, God fulfilled Israel's wish. Even though Israel did not always recognize it, God continued to be Israel's true king, and through the prophets, declared that one day God's reign and rule would recapture Israel's allegiance and then spread to the ends of the earth (Psalm 2).

### God as parent

We have already explored the implications of this image, specifically in relation to often unfaithful Israel. But there is more to be said. We find a fascinating set of questions tucked away near the end of the book of Proverbs.

Who has gone up to heaven and come down?
    Whose hands have gathered up the wind?
Who has wrapped up the waters in a cloak?
    Who has established all the ends of the earth?
What is his name, *and what is the name of his son*?
(Proverbs 30:4, emphasis added)

The Old Testament declares who established the ends of the earth and exercises sovereign control of heaven and earth. That would be God, the great Creator. But this text asks who God's son is. Today we know the answer to the mysterious riddle. It is Jesus!

God was looking for a faithful son. Adam is declared in Scripture to be "son of God" (Luke 3:38), but Adam did not remain faithful, nor did any except Jesus in the human race that has come after him. Solomon was declared to be "son of God" (1 Chronicles 17:13), but he also failed. We have already discussed how Israel often failed to live faithfully as "God's son" (Hosea 11:1). The Old Testament ends without identifying the ultimately faithful Son of God . . . and so it closes with God still portrayed as a faithful parent looking for a faithful son.

That's how things remained until God sent the "only begotten of the Father" to earth and he "became flesh" (John 1:14 NKJV). What a generous, merciful heavenly Father we have. When no faithful "son" can be found, God provides one for us. And so we now also have the privilege of calling God "Abba" (Father). Those who do this learn through Jesus "what great love the Father has lavished on us, that we should be called children of God! And that is what we are!" (1 John 3:1).

Moses describes this wonderful God of Israel:

> I will proclaim the name of the LORD.
> > Oh, praise the greatness of our God!
> He is the Rock, his works are perfect,
> > and all his ways are just.
> A faithful God who does no wrong,
> > upright and just is he.
>
> Is he not your Father, your Creator,
> > who made you and formed you?
> (Deuteronomy 32:3–4, 6)

As we learn to revel in such images of our amazing God, we discover how much more they provide than any abstract doctrinal statements ever could, and we also learn to accept the portraits and images less easily incorporated into our concept of God. Or at least we learn to admit how much we can learn about God from the Old Testament and how much more we can anticipate learning as we encounter Jesus in the New and the triune God in eternity to come.

## PATTERNS OF REWARD AND PUNISHMENT

There are other difficult topics associated with the Old Testament, including punishment, miracles, war, and a multitude of laws. Instead of avoiding these problems, I want to put them openly on the table and share my personal perspectives on them. I confess that the Old Testament (along with the New) is the Word of God, an inspiring narrative of what God really did do in history. And I do that despite the many questions and objections often raised against the Bible and especially against the Old Testament. The rest of this chapter and the next represent my current best attempt to make sense of some of these challenging issues.

Some OT texts say that it will always go well for those who live right, and that terrible things will always follow those who do evil. The strong insistence that this is simply fact flies in the face of a great deal of human experience. Moreover, it flies in the face of many texts in the Old Testament that make claims incompatible with this.

We often affirmingly quote texts like the following: "See, I am setting before you today a blessing and a curse—the blessing if you obey the commands of the LORD your God that I am giving you today; the curse if you disobey the commands of the LORD your God and turn from the way that I command you today by following other gods, which you have not known" (Deuteronomy 11:26–28). "The LORD does not let the righteous go hungry, but he thwarts the craving of the wicked" (Proverbs 10:3). Yet if we are honest, we have to admit that they do not always seem to prove true in experience!

What is an appropriate response to texts like these? First, we need to recognize that speech and writing styles vary greatly from age to age and culture to culture. At times we aim for nuanced and technically accurate speech, and at times we use hyperbole, or we overgeneralize to make an emphatic point, never imagining that our hearers or readers will assume there could never be exceptions.

Moreover, the Old Testament itself emphatically declares that this one pattern does not cover all cases. The reward-and-punishment pattern is especially strong in Deuteronomy, in some psalms, and in the book of Proverbs. But it is strongly challenged, balanced, and nuanced in books like Job. A primary concern of the book of Job is to warn against arguing backward from the fortunes or misfortunes that people face to the assumption that they must have earned their rewards and punishments by good and bad behavior. We see this also in specific texts that directly address the issue at hand.

Take, for example, Psalm 73. The psalmist begins by declaring what he wants to confess, indeed what much of the Old Testament claims: "Surely God is good to Israel, to those who are pure in heart" (73:1). But then he acknowledges that this is, for him, not an assuring word, but a troubling one. It simply does not prove true in his experience. After honest wrestling, and after a new experience in the presence of God, he redefines what "good" means so that he can continue to confess the goodness of God. The final verse declares, "But as for me, it is good to be near God" (73:28).

Texts that promise God's blessing as a reward for our faithfulness play an important, positive function. They encourage us to seek God and God's ways. What they do not do, if we take the larger message of Scripture seriously, is guarantee that the kinds of blessings we desire will come immediately or automatically. God is not portrayed as a vending machine, delivering good things in response to our moral investments. And texts that warn of God's judgment should also not be heard as guaranteed payback for bad behavior. To read them that way is to eviscerate their impact. Anyone who looks around knows that it doesn't always work out this way. Yet the warning texts can play a positive role, encouraging faithful obedience, for indeed, those who live out of sync with God's good purposes will often experience the negative outcomes of doing so, if not immediately, then eventually, and if not in this life, then in the final reckoning.

Life is more complex than any simple reward-and-punishment scheme can capture. God's people in the Old Testament knew that, so they could receive God's instruction, whether it came in black-and-white declarations or in poetic, soul-searching, and paradoxical responses to challenging issues that they had to learn to leave in God's hands. God could be trusted because God was declared to be both merciful and just, even when experience does not *yet* confirm how this will be revealed in the long run.

The problems we have with this are precisely that: *our* problems. We want clear answers and a life without ambiguity. We want to see God's payback, and the sooner the better. Sometimes we need not only the Old Testament's insightful responses to our questions, but its challenge to our priorities. Our goal should be to learn the lessons of each text without immediately forcing them into a system of thought that answers all our questions. The promises of God's blessing should motivate us to follow God's ways as individuals and as communities of faith. The warnings of God's judgment should remind us that our actions have consequences, and that our God is not someone to be messed with. The texts that recognize the suffering of even the most faithful lead us to trust and put our hope in the One who will one day make all things right. And thus the Old Testament looks forward, preparing us for the greater insight into all this that we discover in Jesus.

If we wrestle honestly with the ambiguities of life, we will more easily recognize that the OT authors did the same. They knew that a life lived according to God's will is a rewarding life, and that the reward is sometimes paid out in coins quite different from those the world collects. In the Old Testament we already find the first intimations of what the New Testament makes explicit: "Blessed are you . . . because great is your reward in heaven" (Matthew 5:11–12).

## WONDERFUL AND SOMETIMES STRANGE MIRACLES

Are we expected to believe that an ax head literally floated on the surface of the Jordan River (2 Kings 6:4–7)? Or that a blazing furnace made seven times hotter managed to burn only the ropes binding three men, leaving their lives, their hair, and their clothes untouched, even by the smell (Daniel 3:1–30)? Or that a donkey scolded a prophet (Numbers 22:28–30)? And are we expected to believe that the whole world was flooded with water, right up to and above Mount Everest (Genesis 7:19–20)?

Some readers of both the Old and New Testaments stumble over the many miracle reports found in the Bible. In the opinion of some, such events no longer occur today, and therefore they struggle to believe that such events ever really happened. And for many, once doubt sets in about the biblical miracles, the whole message of Scripture begins to unravel. After all, who wants to build a life on legends and fairy tales?

In the age of modernity and rationalism, a preoccupation in the Western world was to place confidence in whatever scientists declared to be "proven." Against this background, miracle accounts were a big problem. Some of that has dissipated in the age we call postmodernity. Many are willing to admit that we understand the world and its secrets far less clearly than previously thought. If credible witnesses say they have experienced a miracle, why should we doubt it? If it is not *the* truth, at least it might be *their* truth.

This raises new challenges to a Christian worldview. But at least it addresses what I consider to be an unwarranted skepticism about the reality of miracles. We would do well to take scholar N. T. Wright's challenge seriously:

> It may be time to be skeptical about skepticism itself. In Jesus' own day there were plenty of people who didn't want to believe his message, because it would have challenged their own power and influence. For the last two hundred years that's been the mood in the Western society too. . . . Skepticism is no more neutral or objective than faith. . . . Saying this doesn't, of course, prove anything in itself. It just suggests that we keep an open mind and recognize that skepticism too comes with its own agenda.[2]

## THE CASE FOR BELIEVING IN MIRACLES

I believe in miracles, and I am happy to share some of the reasons for this.

- The historical evidence that some miracles happened is (or should be) sufficient to convince most people who do not exclude the possibility of miracles in principle. Take the resurrection of Jesus as an example. Some cheerfully sweep the evidence under the rug with claims like "The supposed 'witnesses' are all dead, so they are useless." Or, "How do we know if he was even really dead?" or, "Isn't that just the kind of thing gullible people might come to believe?" I've found that serious books weighing the historical evidence are often far more credible attempts at getting at the truth than these dismissive statements. Not all of these books depend on prior assumptions about biblical inerrancy, either. The historical evidence for some miracles may not count as incontestable objective proof, but that evidence does contribute to a positive case for miracles if we are willing to take the possibility seriously.

- I believe that the reliability of Scripture is sacrificed if its central narrative (including the claim that Jesus was raised back to life) is not a true account of what God did in history. I understand the point of view of someone who says that floating ax heads don't seem essential to the storyline. But other miracles certainly do. If we have adequate reasons to believe that the Bible is a reliable book, then major miracles have indeed occurred. The two claims stand or fall together.

- The very nature of the gospel depends on believing in a God who truly does intervene in the affairs of this world. The life of Jesus has no adequate explanation if we limit ourselves to the ordinary "laws" of cause and effect. God did something special in the life of Jesus. God had been doing special things for God's people, indeed for all of creation, long before Jesus came, and has been doing so ever since.

- I am convinced that I have personally experienced miracles—not regularly, perhaps none as amazing as many biblical miracles, but God has also intervened in my life. Many other Christians can bear witness to their own experiences of the supernatural. We might be mistaken sometimes. And we may not get miracles whenever we want them. But the fact that they do not *always* occur does not mean miracles *never* happen.

- It is "natural" for miracles to happen. Some argue that the universe is a closed system. Everything works in accordance with laws of cause and effect. God's intervention must be excluded in principle because God designed the world to work by fixed laws. But that's just not true. Every time we make a personal choice to act or not to act, to do this or to do that, we are influencing the course of nature. Only those who claim that humans do not truly make free decisions would dispute this point. If we as humans can interrupt and shape the "natural course" of things, why not God? When we influence something, we simply call it human action. When God does that, we call it divine intervention or a miracle. Both are possible, and both happen. God designed "nature" to interact with "the supernatural."

When the Old Testament includes miracle reports, it is because these events really happened. Yet the miracles themselves often do not seem to be the main concern in the texts that report them. Take, for example, the book of Jonah. We often first learn the story in Sunday school because it is such a great story about the miraculous rescue of a drowning man by a hungry fish and a well-aimed vomit.

That is surely not the main concern of the book. The greatest act of divine intervention and rescue in the book is not the divinely instituted rescue of Jonah; it is the divinely instituted saving of the Ninevites! Indeed, God used a surprising instrument (a great fish) to save Jonah. Even more amazing is that God used a reluctant prophet who didn't really understand God's mercy to bring about the salvation of an entire city, and a city of Gentiles at that. Sometimes the greatest miracles are not those that cause the most amazement or raise the most doubt, but rather those from which we have the most to learn.

## HISTORICAL FACTUALITY AND POETIC LANGUAGE

Old Testament interpreters sometimes struggle to know when historical factuality matters and when it does not. Sometimes it is pretty obvious. When Isaiah 55:12 refers to trees clapping their hands, it would be quite a stretch to imagine that God will one day miraculously intervene to give hands to trees so that they can do that. Otherwise, the text does not speak truthfully, and therefore cannot be divine revelation. No! It's an expression, a moving, important, meaningful one.

Elsewhere, things are less obvious. Does the message of the text depend on its literal factuality? Sometimes we cannot easily parse out which aspects of God's engagement involve what we call natural events, and which were uniquely divine interventions. Some of the plagues of Egypt, for example, sound like unusually large epidemics. Does God sometimes use events of nature and sometimes intervene directly? The Bible employs a lot of imagery, quite a lot of hyperbole, and sometimes sagas. It also reports divine interventions. If we cannot always be sure into which category a text falls, that does not detract from the main point: God is actively engaged in creation in a multitude of ways, including those events that we call miracles.

Nineteenth-century evangelist George Müller is reported to have said, "God can use ordinary events in such a way that they become miracles." Some biblical accounts are reported as miracles, even though there may well have been what we call a "natural explanation" for whatever occurred. We neither know nor need to know exactly how God worked in some situations.

In summary, God has worked and continues to work miraculously. We do not have complete clarity concerning precisely how God intervened in many situations. The reliability of the Bible does not depend on whether we can identify exactly where the historical factuality in a text ends and where the telling of artistic, instructive, and edifying stories begins. We cannot judge OT historians by our criteria. In their time, historical exactness was less important than presenting what we might call an "authoritative insider perspective."[3]

Insiders in OT times were often inspired prophets who were granted special insight into what God was doing. They were fully aware that God does miracles, sometimes even stupendous, history-changing miracles. God cares about humanity and God's set-apart people. We may not fully understand all the texts that reveal this, but a good starting point is to trust them.

## WHY SHOULD WE ENGAGE DIFFICULT TOPICS IN THE OLD TESTAMENT?

We have addressed some challenging topics, and more are to come. Some Bible readers would rather ignore these issues. Others are so troubled by them that they cannot get past them and then lose confidence that the Bible is worth reading and studying. My hope is that these reflections encourage continued study.

We may not gain full clarity on some of the issues, but our deep wrestling with Scripture will honor God, will follow the model of Jesus and the early church, and will lead us to encounter rich treasures in that part of the Bible we call the Old Testament.

# Questions for discussion

1. Have you had experiences with abstract formulations and doctrines of God similar to those described in the chapter? Or have you found such formulations and doctrines to be helpful? Which of the images and portraits of God in the Old Testament are particularly meaningful to you as you reflect on your experience of God?

2. Which OT resources help you as you wrestle with the seemingly unfair distribution of good and evil in human experience? How does the further revelation of God and God's plans and purposes through Jesus provide additional resources for dealing with these challenging issues?

3. What convictions do you hold and what questions do you have about divine interventions? Is it important to you to be able to identify precisely when God's activity should be considered a "miracle"? Why or why not?

# TOO MUCH WAR AND TOO MANY LAWS

*You have heard that it was said, "Love your neighbor and hate your enemy." But I tell you, love your enemies and pray for those who persecute you, that you may be children of your Father in heaven. He causes his sun to rise on the evil and the good, and sends rain on the righteous and the unrighteous."*
—Matthew 5:43–45

Matthew 5 speaks directly to the topics of war and the law. Most of Jesus' contemporaries were sure they knew what the Messiah would do when he arrived. He would lead Israel into battle and defeat the Romans. When Jesus announced the arrival of God's kingdom but then told his followers to love their enemies ("What? You mean the Romans?"), many felt justified in rejecting Jesus as just another messianic pretender. They thought they understood the "warring God" of their Scriptures. They were not prepared to let Jesus question that image!

Yet Jesus does precisely that by reinterpreting the law for his followers. He challenges their previous understanding by teaching in contrast, "You have heard . . . But I say . . ." Jesus rejects scribal misinterpretations of the law and sometimes revises what the Old Testament commands or prohibits. Jesus paves the way for the later church to do the same.

Christians today desperately need NT insight, and especially Jesus' own teaching, to address challenging topics in the Old Testament. In particular, we need to rethink war and violence and the role of law.

❖

The previous chapter addressed three issues that sometimes make it difficult for Christian readers of the Old Testament to connect with it: its sometimes questionable portraits of God; its reward-and-punishment perspective; and its sometimes hard-to-believe miracle accounts. In this chapter I engage two other challenging topics.

## TOO MUCH WAR

The OT perspective on war is particularly challenging for those in what is sometimes called the "peace church" tradition, a label often applied to denominations and Christians who, because of their conviction that peacemaking is central to the gospel, advocate for alternatives to military participation.

But the challenge of understanding the OT perspective on war is there for all Bible readers, regardless of personal persuasions about contemporary military engagement. In fact, the tension between what the Old Testament seems to endorse and what the New Testament in general and Jesus in particular teach provides a significant challenge to those who confess that the entire Bible is authoritative for faith and practice.

The God revealed to us in Jesus Christ is a God of peace, a God who loves not only friends, but also enemies. How can it then be that the same God in earlier times commanded God's people to completely destroy whole people groups (Deuteronomy 7:1–2)? Did God really fight for or with Israel and enable them to defeat powerful enemies? There are two common but very different approaches to understanding this.

One approach starts with the conviction that war is so abhorrent that a righteous and loving God could not possibly endorse it. Because the Old Testament claims that God sometimes does endorse war, this approach leads to rejecting the Old Testament along with the "war-mongering God" that it apparently presents to us. If the Old Testament really does promote war as a divine strategy for managing international relations and for favoring one people group over all the others, it is tempting to simply declare the Old Testament wrong, and thus not to be received as reliable divine revelation.

The other approach starts at the opposite end. Its nonnegotiable conviction is that the Bible is from beginning to end trustworthy divine revelation, revealing the perfect will of God. Since God endorses warfare as a divinely ordained strategy for defense, judgment, and even conquest, we must simply accept that military action, even for the people of God—perhaps especially for the people of God—and for the nations where they have considerable influence, is fully consistent with God's work in this world.

What if both approaches oversimplify the situation? What if the Old Testament does *not* promote aggressive military action to gain or safeguard national advantages? And what if what the Old Testament *does* say about war is not at all directly applicable to issues of modern warfare? That would change the way we approach the topic of war in the Old Testament. I suggest some observations to keep in mind.

1. No straight line can be drawn from Israel's battles in the Old Testament to modern warfare in our day. It is not

uncommon for Christians, especially in the United States, to draw a straight line from Israel's battles to modern warfare: "If God commanded Israel to go to battle against God's enemies, then it is appropriate for this country to go to war against its enemies." But that approach makes three wrong assumptions:

- That the coming of Christ did nothing to change this perspective.
- That our allegiance to our country should supersede our allegiance to all God's people, worldwide, on both sides of every military engagement.
- That "Israel" in the Old Testament somehow corresponds to "the United States" now.

A very great deal did in fact change with the coming of Jesus. No straight line should ever be drawn from anything in the Old Testament to modern-day application without considering how the coming of Jesus shapes what an appropriate application should look like.

As to allegiance—in the Old Testament, God's covenant community was *embedded within* but not equal to Israel as a nation. The NT expansion of God's covenant community into the Gentile world means it is embedded and fully at home within *every people group and nation* the gospel has reached. If our final allegiance is to Christ and the people of God, that must affect how we view the national ambitions of all nations, including our own. At the very least it must erase any direct line we draw between ancient Israel and our country today. That then also refutes the third assumption listed above.

We should read and interpret the OT texts about warfare carefully, first on their own terms and then in the light of the whole canon of Christian Scripture. When we do that, I propose that we note at least the following additional points.

2. Not all wars that Israel fought corresponded to God's will. We misread the Old Testament if we assume that Israel fought wars always and only in obedience to God's command. Only a minority of the referenced battles were ordered by God. Israel had demanded a king precisely so they would have someone to lead them into battle (1 Samuel 8:20). Though God gave in to their demands, God never intended either the monarchy or the wars to which it led them.

The dominant viewpoint in the ancient Near East was that each people group had their own god or gods, who endorsed and supported the wars they fought. Victory in battle was viewed not only as humans beating humans, but as one god defeating another. The enemies of each people group were automatically the enemies of the local gods who ruled them (and vice versa). Israel, however, should always have known better. Enemies of Israel were not necessarily enemies of Israel's God, for Israel's God was and is the God of the whole earth.

God sometimes used Israel to punish other nations in the time of the Old Testament, but God also used other nations to punish Israel. Attempts to draw principles from the Old Testament for modern national ambitions do not work nearly as well when this is considered. We should always assume that when Israel declared war on neighboring peoples, it was likely their own initiative and not God's intentions, unless the texts clearly say otherwise.

3. God can use the results of war to fulfill divine purposes. God is able to fulfill divine purposes *despite* and sometimes even *through* the wrong choices people make and the evil deeds they do. God can use what God neither initiates nor endorses. A German expression translates into "Even on crooked lines, God can write straight!"[1] That applies to the lives of individuals and to the lives of nations.

International treaties, conflicts between nations, power shifts between empires, and other historical events can be used by God to influence the course of history for whole people groups. We remind ourselves of Joseph's assessment of his own life, when he tells his brothers: "You intended to harm me, but God intended it for good to accomplish what is now being done, the saving of many lives" (Genesis 50:20).

God is also a righteous God who holds accountable those who misuse power, even if in the end God makes something good come out of what they initiate. Some OT wars are portrayed as God's promise-keeping to one nation and simultaneously God's act of judgment on one that had departed so far from God's purposes that they were ripe for God's judgment. Both aspects are consistent with God's larger OT plan, and both contribute to bringing that plan closer to completion.

4. The Old Testament focuses more directly on the collective than on the individual. In NT times and today, attention is paid to individual rights and fairness for the individual in ways virtually unheard of in ancient times. Back in OT times, individuals were seen as constituent elements of something larger. Just as hurricanes and tsunamis strike whatever and whoever is in their path, so also God's righteous anger in the Old Testament seems to deal with whole people groups, regardless of individual righteous persons within them.

A whole people group could be punished for their unfaithfulness (Jeremiah 12:17). The innocent suffered because of and along with the guilty. Correspondingly, God sometimes used Israel in battle to punish whole people groups (not specifically each individual within them). A people group that hated the God of Israel was destroyed (Deuteronomy 7:1–2, 10). A city that gave itself over to idolatry was destroyed (13:12–16).

Families were punished along with the one guilty person (Joshua 7:24–25; 1 Samuel 3:13).

There are exceptions to this pattern. God was willing to negotiate with Abraham before punishing Sodom. God would have spared even the guilty if there had been ten righteous people in the city.

The additional issue of divine justice for the individual is not often addressed in the Old Testament. When it is addressed, new interpretive challenges arise, for some texts seem to affirm what others seem to deny. Theologians have always struggled with the question of divine justice. The Old Testament tends to defer clarity and simply declare, "God is God! There are some things we will not be able to understand about God's ways."

That seems to be a large part of Job's message. As observed in the previous chapter, it is also the perspective of Psalm 73. The psalmist wrestles directly with why good things happen to bad people. The psalmist concludes that the theological dilemma this question evokes looks very different if we consider God's *final* judgment when justice will ultimately be done.

By far the most helpful perspectives on this question come to us from the pages of the New Testament, specifically in the life, death, and resurrection of Jesus. God suffers with us when we suffer. What happens in this life is only part of the story. When we see God face-to-face, there will be answers to the theological and experiential struggles that often plague us now.

5. There are counter-voices within the Old Testament. Sometimes we have the impression that in OT times, war simply belonged to the assumptions about how the world works. But significant texts call this into question. Some texts sound as though it really was Israel's assignment to obliterate whole people groups who were living in the promised land (see Deuteronomy 7:1–3), but other texts give the impression that God

had always intended for Israel to live at peace alongside other people groups in the same geographic area.

Israel's role was to model a just society so others would be drawn to the God of Israel. "When a foreigner resides among you in your land, do not mistreat them. The foreigner residing among you must treated as your native-born. Love them as yourself, for you were foreigners in Egypt. I am the LORD your God" (Leviticus 19:33–34). In their treatment of others among them, Israel would be a contrast society. Love of enemies was already introduced as God's will thousands of years before Jesus.

Though some texts may give the impression that God's anger strikes hard and swiftly when humans deserve God's punishment, other texts emphasize the other side of the coin. God is a patient and merciful God! "His anger lasts only a moment, but his favor lasts a lifetime" (Psalm 30:5). God even sent prophets to neighboring cities so that people there would be called to repentance and thus avoid God's judgment (see the book of Jonah).

Some texts create the impression that war and violence, though perhaps unavoidable in this fallen world, do not correspond to God's real purposes. One day God's real intentions for humanity will be realized and war shall be no more. The prophet Micah speaks to this hope: "He will judge between many peoples and will settle disputes for strong nations far and wide. They will beat their swords into plowshares and their spears into pruning hooks. Nation will not take up sword against nation, nor will they train for war anymore" (Micah 4:3). Whether this hope is intended already for life in this world or only for the world to come, this prophetic message reveals God's perfect will. Those who carry this hope in their hearts seek to live toward its realization already now.

As we read through the Old Testament, the voices that call for peaceful coexistence between nations speak louder and louder, and earlier emphases on one nation defeating or exterminating the other seem to fade away. During the time of Israel's exile in Babylon, the prophet Jeremiah goes so far as to advise Israel to relinquish its own national aspirations, at least temporarily. This time God did not intend for Israel to gain its freedom through military conquest. On the contrary, Israel was to seek the shalom of the foreign cities where they had been forcibly resettled. "Seek the peace and prosperity of the city to which I have carried you into exile. Pray to the LORD for it, because if it prospers, you too will prosper" (Jeremiah 29:7). God would ensure that Israel returned to its homeland without starting a revolution or winning a battle.

The monarchy, established against God's will, was a direct or indirect contributor to a great deal of Israel's ancient warfare. Shifts in the monarchy often corresponded to shifts in attitudes to violence. In the time of the patriarchs Abraham, Isaac, and Jacob, the dominant approach to conflict was nonviolent negotiation. At the time of Israel's rescue from Egypt, God acted unilaterally, not involving Israel at all in the victory that set them free. At that time, war was regularly "Yahweh's war." During the conquest, Israel was involved in many of the battles, but the battles themselves were defined as God's victories. This changed significantly after the institution of the monarchy.

Old Testament scholar Millard Lind points out that the growing desire of Israel for a king corresponded to Israel's growing self-sufficiency. They relied more and more on their own strength, trusting God less and less for their security. They wanted a king like all the other nations so that their king could lead them into battle. Lind writes, "The order founded upon Yahweh's miracle was exchanged for an order that moved toward the human manipulation and control of political resources involving violent power."[2]

We find two tendencies during the time of the monarchy. In those texts where the monarchy is most strongly criticized, military victories are mostly ascribed to God. In those texts that seem to favor the monarchy, miracles seem to be downplayed, and victories are credited to the king.[3] Two alternative viewpoints are promoted, but when we read the prophetic literature, the first of these is the one corresponding to God's will. The nations themselves are called to beat their swords into plowshares.

6. Jesus corrects all inadequate portraits of God, including the portrait of a warring God. God came to us in Jesus. One of the purposes of the incarnation was that God might be revealed to us more clearly than had been possible before. Biblical portraits of God drawn from the Old Testament need to be reexamined in the light of Jesus' presence, for in Jesus they are clarified, completed, or even corrected. When a particular view of God is gained from the content of the Old Testament but stands in tension with what we see more clearly in Jesus Christ, then the NT portrait should always be given priority.

The New Testament reveals to us a God who loves all people, who is merciful and generous with all. In Jesus we see this God embodied. Jesus lived in such a way that God's love, generosity, and forgiveness were freely offered to all. Jesus himself said that God "causes his sun to rise on the evil and the good, and sends rain on the righteous and the unrighteous" (Matthew 5:45). This is precisely where Jesus emphatically states that his followers are to love their enemies (see 5:44). Instead of drawing from the OT portraits of a warring God, a presumed justification for hating or killing our enemies, we should draw from Jesus a clearer picture and model of our God, who calls us to love enemies as God does.

Theologians speak of "progressive revelation." As we read through the Bible, we gain clarity about who God is and how God's plan is to be fulfilled. The earlier pictures in Scripture do not qualify on their own as "the biblical view." We need the teaching and the model of Jesus if we want to claim to have understood God as revealed by the Bible. In Jesus and with the New Testament, God has allowed us to see more clearly what God is really like: a God who loves all people and calls us to do the same, even when doing so costs us our lives. We are called to follow the victorious slain Lamb who shows us the way *into*, and the way *of*, God's final kingdom of peace.

## TOO MANY LAWS

The OT books Exodus, Leviticus, Numbers, and Deuteronomy seem to be full of laws: this must be done; that must be avoided; if this happens, people should respond like this. For example: "If anyone's bull injures someone else's bull and it dies, the two parties are to sell the live one and divide both the money and the dead animal equally" (Exodus 21:35). Countless guidelines describe how an animal should be slaughtered in a sacrifice and how the presiding priest should be dressed (Leviticus 1:3–12; Exodus 28:1–43). It seems unending. Who can appreciate the religion of the Old Testament when it seems to be nothing but rules?

In light of this, isn't it amazing that the ancient Israelites seem to have loved the law with all their hearts? At least the psalmist gives this impression: "Oh, how I love your law! I meditate on it all day long" (Psalm 119:97). "I hate double-minded people, but I love your law" (119:113). *They* understood that God had given them the law to help them live better lives. It is *we* who seem to find all these laws problematic. To us, the laws seem too numerous, too restrictive, and often completely irrelevant. Therefore we must think carefully about the function of all these laws in the life of the Israelites and in ours. I propose ten points for consideration:

1. To start, we have far more laws than they had! According to the rabbis, the Books of Moses contain about 613 laws. I live in California, where we have a drivers handbook containing about 850 rules. I also checked the National Football League rulebook: It contains about 950 rules in the rulebook section, and an additional 1,200 or so in the casebook section. Sometimes we find a few of the traffic laws inconvenient. Sometimes we wish they could just "get on with the game." But would we really want to dispense with most of these rules? There would be chaos on the streets and on the football field. We learn to live with *all these rules* and the thousands more that regulate other aspects of life, and we usually consider them good. We don't meditate on the *California Driver's Handbook* or express our love for the NFL rulebook the way we would the Bible, but then, they are not God-given and designed to bring peace and wholeness to the whole human family and to please God.

2. Not all laws are about ethical issues. Old Testament "laws" speak not only to religious and ethical issues, but also address legal, social, and national matters. "Israel" at the time was both the covenant people of God and a nation-state. The Spirit guided the early church to declare most of the OT social, cultural, and national laws irrelevant for the church, or at least for Gentiles within it. That became evident the instant the church discerned that one does not need to be a Jew to be a Christian.[4]

3. Many of the OT laws, even some ethical guidelines, were only for the people of Israel. Some of the OT commands and

prohibitions apply always and everywhere. An example would be the Ten Commandments, which are cited repeatedly in the New Testament. But many others do not have permanent binding authority. This is not because "the age of grace" has now replaced "the age of law," as some falsely claim. It is not because the laws were always for them (Israel) and not for us (church), as others falsely claim. Rather, some commands and prohibitions really were limited to certain times and places based on historical-cultural context, or one's place within ongoing salvation history.

There is no simple formula to discern which laws still apply and which do not. The most important principle to observe is that God did not issue rules and regulations arbitrarily; they were designed to achieve important goals in God's overall plan for humanity and for Israel in particular. If we focus on God's nature and God's purposes, we can often discern wisely which laws still apply to us directly, and when God may be aiming to achieve the same underlying goals but in different ways.

4. Sometimes the rules, and especially the prohibitions, were designed to keep God's people from idolatry. The more we learn about ancient religious practices, the more likely it seems that some things were forbidden not because they were intrinsically evil, but because they belonged to the religious customs of neighboring peoples and could easily have led God's people into pagan worship. Paul's instructions not to attend feasts in pagan temples (e.g., 1 Corinthians 8:9-13) is something comparable that we find in the New Testament. We can learn from such prohibitions, but they do not specify which cultural events we should perhaps avoid for similar reasons today.

5. Sometimes the OT laws concerned meaningful economic or health measures. Some of the kosher food laws may seem arbitrary to us, but scientists have discovered that often they

made good sense in the agricultural and climate conditions of the Israelites' time and place. In a context without refrigeration where other means of food preservation were less developed than today, avoiding certain foods would have had considerable health benefits. God wanted to save the people from harm and sometimes prohibited dangerous or wasteful things, whether the Israelites always understand the reasons or not.

6. Sometimes we just do not understand. Israel probably did not understand God's reasoning behind some of the commands and prohibitions. For example, in Leviticus 19:18 we find the very important and permanently binding command "Love your neighbor as yourself." In the very next verse we find prohibitions that seem irrelevant to us: "Do not plant your field with two kinds of seed. Do not wear clothing woven of two kinds of material" (19:19). Does this have something to do with fertility religions or with avoiding forbidden magic? We just don't know. We cannot always determine why some things are labeled "detestable things the LORD hates" (Deuteronomy 12:31). God loved the covenant people, therefore all the commands and prohibitions that applied to them would have been for their benefit. We should assume that the same is true today, whether or not we understand the purposes of individual commands and prohibitions.

7. Animal sacrifices played an important role at the time, but no longer do today. There are some similarities between the sacrifices that God required and those practiced by Israel's pagan neighbors. Yet pagan sacrifice often seemed like a desperate attempt to win the favor of a selfish and vindictive god. Israel was being taught through the sacrificial system that God is a gracious God, eager to forgive, accepting a substitute in place of the guilty, the helpless, and the defiled.

The Old Testament prepares us through its system of sacrifices to recognize the grace of God exercised in Jesus, the
willing sacrifice, the Lamb of God who takes away the sin
of the world. Animal sacrifices are forever eliminated by their
fulfillment in Jesus. The church instead celebrates the communion service (the Lord's Supper), symbolizing the meaning of
Jesus' death and the new life it provides.

8. The laws themselves were never the focus of the relationship between God and God's people. As discussed in chapter
5 of this book, God's covenant with Israel was based on a
relationship of fidelity. Laws play a subordinate and supporting role.

9. The law is not given just to expose sin. The law does
indeed expose sin (see Romans 7:7) and lead us to Jesus, who
wipes the slate clean. But because this was not the law's only
task and not even the most important one, we must not imagine that the Old Testament is primarily about dos and don'ts.
God's law has always been God's gift to guide God's people in
wholesome, life-giving, and God-pleasing ways.

10. The main role of the law has always been to reveal
God's will to God's people. If we live our lives in accordance
with God's instructions, our lives will be pleasing to God, and
God will bless us abundantly. If we consider points 1–9, the
challenge of understanding the commands and prohibitions is
brought into perspective. When I was a child listening to my
father read scripture around the breakfast table, I sighed with
relief when long genealogies finally ended, only to sigh anew
when the topic shifted to how priests should be clothed, or
how the tabernacle should be decorated.

However, if we are willing to view the Old Testament's
many instructions as part of the history of a people in whom
we also find our spiritual roots, then even long lists of dos

and don'ts can draw us to appreciate how our God guides us in the details of life and how God used OT laws to prepare a people to recognize and receive the Christ. Jesus came not so that all the laws would go away, but to fulfill the law and to give us the Holy Spirit, who writes God's laws upon our hearts (Jeremiah 31:33). And so we can also say, "Oh, how I love your law! I meditate on it all day long" (Psalm 119:97). That would be a worthy goal, wouldn't it?

## CAN WE STILL VALUE THE OLD TESTAMENT DESPITE ITS WARFARE AND COUNTLESS LAWS?

We can and we must, for Jesus did and he is our model. In terms of warfare and peacemaking, Jesus emphasized certain perspectives, relativized others, reversed and carried forward still others. We interpret the OT texts in their original contexts, and then exercise careful discernment about how and when to apply the lessons learned to our context. When we do, we see a strong shift from warfare to peacemaking, especially for followers of Jesus.

And we see that OT law was not designed to be a burden, but a gift. Much of it still applies. Much of it does not. Jesus and the New Testament are our guides.

# *Questions for discussion*

---

1.  "If our final allegiance is to Christ and the people
    of God, that must affect how we view the national
    ambitions of all nations, including our own. At
    the very least it must erase any direct line we draw
    between ancient Israel and our country today." How
    do you respond to this claim? How do your convic-
    tions about this influence your views on the relation-
    ship between "divine warfare" in the Old Testament
    and modern wars fought today?

2.  "Instead of drawing from the OT portraits of a
    warring God, a presumed justification for hating or
    killing our enemies, we should draw from Jesus a
    clearer picture and model of our God, who calls us to
    love enemies as God does." What are the implications
    of doing what this quotation proposes?

3.  Which of the ten observations about law (ancient
    and modern) do you find particularly persuasive or
    helpful as you discern the relevance of OT laws for
    Christians today?

# READING AND UNDERSTANDING THE OLD TESTAMENT

*Everything must be fulfilled that is written about me in the Law of Moses, the Prophets and the Psalms.* —Luke 24:44

During Jesus' earthly ministry, he regularly fulfilled OT prophecies about what would happen when the Messiah arrived and God showed up in person to live among the people of God.

Now the resurrected Jesus helps his followers understand that even his own death and resurrection align with what the Old Testament taught, and that these were necessary preconditions for the very existence of the believing community that would now fulfill Israel's mission: bringing God's good news to the whole world.

The whole OT story finds its culmination and goal in Jesus. And Jesus is the one who teaches us to read and understand that story.

❖

Along with the apostle Paul, we confess:

> Every Scripture is God-breathed and profitable for teach-
> ing, for reproof, for correction, and for instruction in
> righteousness, that each person who belongs to God may
> be complete, thoroughly equipped for every good work.
> (2 Timothy 3:16–17 WEB)

This text refers to that collection of books we now call the
Old Testament. The books making up the New Testament had
not yet been written, collected, and canonized. Christians now
confess that 2 Timothy 3:16–17 also applies to what we call
the New Testament, and thus to the whole Christian Bible. All
sixty-six books are now recognized as Holy Scripture, given to
us by God to equip us for good work. These Scriptures have
a very practical function: to make it possible for us to live in
such a way that God is pleased.

What the 2 Timothy text does *not* claim is that every part of
Scripture functions in *the same way*; rather, each contributes
to this common goal. It is often hard to see *how* individual
texts contribute to that overall goal, especially if we fail to
see how each contributes to the larger narrative. Some Bible
readers oversimplify the process, taking individual texts out of
context and squeezing from them a "word from the Lord" for
their own need. But when we do that, we can be led seriously
astray about what the Scriptures teach.

Many of the commands, promises, prohibitions, and encour-
agements found in Scripture played a very significant role in
the lives of those to whom they were originally addressed. If
we thought every one of them applied directly to each of us in
very different circumstances, though, we would certainly run
into great difficulties putting that conviction into practice.

Not every individual *sentence* in Scripture is immediately useful for teaching, rebuking, and correcting. Not every genealogy trains us in righteousness. Not every chronicle of ancient kings is equally helpful for doctrinal study or devotional reading. However, the Old Testament, taken *as a whole*, and the numerous smaller parts that comprise it—narratives, prophecies, instruction, teaching, songs—help us discover God's larger purposes, our role within them, and how we can be shaped and trained to be those coworkers God designed us to be.

Two questions guide our examination of various OT literature: How were these parts of the Old Testament meant to be taken in ancient times? How do they still contribute to our lives so that we "may be thoroughly equipped for every good work"?

## THE THREE-PART BIBLE

Jesus said, "Everything must be fulfilled that is written about me in the Law of Moses, the Prophets and the Psalms." Luke the author then adds, "Then he opened their minds so they could understand the Scriptures" (Luke 24:44–45). Luke's key word *Scriptures* refers to what we now call the Old Testament. Jesus' key terms *Law of Moses*, *Prophets*, and *Psalms* specify the three parts of that collection.

- The Law of Moses refers to what was otherwise called the Pentateuch, or the Books of Moses (Genesis, Exodus, Leviticus, Numbers, and Deuteronomy). The Hebrew word for this set of books is Torah.
- The Prophets refers to the writings of the so-called major prophets (Isaiah, Jeremiah, and Ezekiel), to the Book of the Twelve (Hosea, Joel, Amos, Obadiah, Jonah, Micah, Nahum, Habakkuk, Zephaniah, Haggai, Zechariah,

and Malachi), and then to some of the books we often call history books (Joshua, Judges, 1–2 Samuel, and 1–2 Kings). The Hebrew word for these books is Nevi'im.

- The Psalms stands representatively for a diverse collection of books also known as the Writings or wisdom literature. In this category the Jews included, besides the Psalms, Ruth, Esther, Job, Proverbs, Ecclesiastes, Song of Songs, Lamentations, and interestingly, another set of books we often call history books—Chronicles, Ezra and Nehemiah—and finally Daniel, a book that Christian Bibles include among the Prophets. The Hebrew word for this collection is Ketuvim.

Taken together, the three Hebrew words Torah, Nevi'im, Ketuvim form a common shorthand for the Hebrew Bible: TaNaK (often written as Tanak).

The ancient Hebrews did not label any of their scriptures "history books." That communicates something important. Though historical events are narrated in large portions of the Old Testament, the goal of the texts is not reached when we learn history. If we ask only what really happened, we run the risk of missing the intentions of the text. God's people were to recognize in real historical events something beyond mere historicity. They were to learn the lessons of history for present and future life with God. And they were to recognize the hand of God at work, leading Israel and all creation. The texts were written to equip God's people to be God's coworkers in bringing about God's will on earth as it is in heaven.

## THE GRAND NARRATIVE

The entire Old Testament is a grand narrative, or more accurately, a large part of a narrative even grander than the OT story on its own. It is the story of God's dealings with creation, with humanity, and then particularly with and through God's chosen people, Israel. Countless smaller narratives combine to tell the story. Embedded within these are the laws, prophetic words, psalms, and other contributing parts.

Sometimes the "smaller stories" taken on their own do not seem to make any significant contribution to our being "thoroughly equipped for every good work." Now we switch metaphors from "grand narrative" to "theater production." Countless comments, glances, and actions by the major characters of a theater production (not to mention minor contributions by a host of secondary characters) all contribute to the larger plot and its effect on the audience. In the same way, all the smaller parts of the grand narrative of Scripture contribute to help us grasp the awesome story of God and humanity told by Scripture. Behind all that occurs, God is at work.

In a theater production the actors and the props have their own significance, but if there were no plot and no director coordinating the parts, indeed if there were no script for the play in the first place, it would be impossible for the individual actors to "tell the story."

Yet the drama of biblical history is not *exactly* like a theater production. In the first place it tells a true story, the truest story there is! Theater productions do not always aim to do that. Second, God plays many roles: scriptwriter, director, occasional offstage voice, always acting through characters and occasionally even alongside them onstage. As scriptwriter and director, God is also unique. The goal of the production and some key plotlines are revealed to the actors in advance, but the performers are given astonishing freedom to improvise onstage, both in their speech and in their actions.

At the best of times, the actors on the stage recognize the intended plot development. They speak lines and carry out actions that further that plot. At other times they deviate from what the scriptwriter and director intended as their role. And then God is the one who improvises, finding new ways to further the plot, sometimes replacing actors with those who contribute more faithfully. If we are attentive to this, we see it rather often in biblical history.

The book of Esther, for example, reveals more than most OT books how various faithful and unfaithful characters further God's intended plot. Yet in the entire book of Esther, God is never explicitly named, neither generically ("God") nor by any of God's names. Is God absent? Not at all. God is directing the plot development and using both faithful and unfaithful actors on the stage to move the production forward and communicate with the observing audience. Some characters act in direct opposition to God's intended plot for Israel and the world. Some are faithful. And even after Israel is rescued from danger, Israel departs once more from God's intended role for this major actor.

Other metaphors illustrate how this works. Each brushstroke of a master painter may seem meaningless on its own, but each contributes an essential detail to the landscape or the portrait that graces the canvas. Each note of an oratorio may seem unimportant, but without those "unimportant notes" there would be nothing to hear, let alone the grand performance that musicians, following a great musical score and a master conductor, can produce together.

## CHARACTERS WHO TEACH US

One way that God communicates to readers of Scripture is through individual characters' speeches and actions. Yet exactly how this works is not always self-evident. These characters are both "good" and "bad" (and everything between), and we are not always told explicitly whether their actions are approved by God or considered wrong. For example, did the warrior Jephthah do right or wrong when he kept an oath to God by sacrificing his daughter (see Judges 11:30–39)? Ancient readers may have praised him for paying such a high price to keep his oath. Yet surely, in the light of Jesus' teaching and example, we should conclude that his oath-making was foolish and his oath-keeping utterly wrong.

Some texts appear surprising or even disturbing to us from our vantage point today, but when we consider the conventions and assumptions of the ancient world, we are able to read these texts in a different light. God required a higher standard from Israel than the surrounding nations were practicing, but that higher standard did not necessarily correspond to the even higher standard we see revealed in Jesus and the New Testament. Jesus himself said that because of the hardness of people's hearts, God tolerated and regulated various practices in ancient times that were not consistent with God's perfect will (see Mark 10:5–6). Jesus now calls us to live by God's revealed will, often saying, "You have heard that it was said . . . But I tell you . . ." (Matthew 5:21–22).

After considering the Old Testament *as a whole*, it is time to turn separately to the three categories of scripture to which Jesus referred: the Law of Moses, the Prophets, and the Psalms.

## TRAINING FOR COVENANT FAITHFULNESS

This book has examined the role of the law several times. Here I suggest a series of points to help readers know how best to approach the first five books of the Bible, commonly referred to as the Books of Moses.

First, these five books contain a great deal more than "law." The first seventy chapters of the Bible (Genesis 1–Exodus 20, covered in chapters 1–5 of this book) narrate in a fast-paced and gripping way the origins of human civilization on earth and the stages of human history leading up through the birth of the Israelite people, followed by the developments of this people group up to the point where they are formally bound to God in a covenant of mutual faithfulness. These chapters contain relatively few laws and commandments. What characterizes them is mostly theology embedded in narrative form.

Second, a very large number of laws, commands, prohibitions, and ordinances were intended for specific circumstances. An obvious example would be the numerous explicit instructions for constructing the tabernacle. Once that tabernacle was complete, their prescriptive function was no longer needed. Some interpreters find in virtually every minute detail of these plans symbolic allusions to features of the spiritual life that need to be discerned and practiced in the Christian church. It seems wiser to limit ourselves to those made explicit in Scripture, such as the connections made in the book of Hebrews (Hebrews 8:1–6; 9:1–10:14), thus focusing on general principles of worship and sacrifice. If we create allegorical readings of text designed primarily as a construction blueprint, we can depart far from the intended meanings. The same applies to a host of other detailed texts that instruct the Israelites for specific situations, like their desert wanderings or the clothing of their priests.

Third, many instructions in the Old Testament were designed to regulate religious practices that are explicitly discontinued in an NT context. Most prominent here would be the whole system of slaughtering animals, along with accompanying ceremonies. A designated priesthood administered these at sacred altars, and eventually at the temple in

Jerusalem. For Jews who did not accept Jesus as their Messiah, this system ceased when Jerusalem was destroyed in 70 AD. By that time Christians had already understood that the OT sacrificial system had reached its goal when Jesus fulfilled its deepest meaning through his death on the cross. When we now read those OT texts that speak of animal sacrifices, we can still learn about God's gracious provision of forgiveness and cleansing, but we no longer read those texts as prescriptions for our religious observances.

One way we look back and remember Jesus' sacrifice is in celebrating Christian communion, where we bear witness to Christ's sacrificial death accomplished once and for all. But the NT book that most connects the OT sacrificial system to its fulfillment in Jesus, Hebrews, does not see in Christian communion services the greatest fulfillment of the sacrificial system. Rather, the author exhorts the church to sacrificial *living*: "Through Jesus, therefore, let us continually offer to God a sacrifice of praise—the fruit of lips that openly profess his name. And do not forget to do good and to share with others, for with such sacrifices God is pleased" (13:15–16).

Fourth, many commands and prohibitions that applied to Jews in the time before Jesus' coming are explicitly declared irrelevant for Gentiles by the Jerusalem Council, as reported to us in Acts 15. The issue addressed there was whether Jews and Gentiles could be joined together in one Christian church without following the same requirements. Apostles, elders, and the church as a whole discerned that neither Jews nor Gentiles are ultimately brought into a reconciled relationship with God by carefully observing the prescriptions and prohibitions that had once governed the religious life of faithful Jews. Salvation is by grace, and believers are therefore free to ignore a whole host of guidelines previously required of God's people.

James voiced the group's conclusion: "It is my judgment, therefore, that we should not make it difficult for the Gentiles who are turning to God" (Acts 15:19). What this means is that OT laws governing circumcision, food production and consumption, clothing, and a host of other matters are simply irrelevant for Gentile Christians (and in most cases probably for Jews as well, though the text does not make this explicit).[1]

Finally, the Ten Commandments are presented in the Old Testament as covenant stipulations that define the expected behavior of God's people in the Old Testament. Authors of the New Testament continue to refer to and quote them often, always assuming that they remain in force for all Christians (Jew and Gentile). Yet the New Testament does more than repeat and enforce them. At various points the meaning is deepened and the application broadened.

Even more central than the Ten Commandments are the two great commandments, formulated several times in the New Testament, sometimes by Jesus, sometimes by others. This version is found in Matthew 22:37–39: "Jesus replied: 'Love the Lord your God with all your heart and with all your soul and with all your mind.' This is the first and greatest commandment. And the second is like it: 'Love your neighbor as yourself.'"

Elsewhere, Jesus speaks of "the more important matters of the law—justice, mercy and faithfulness" (Matthew 23:23). These priorities are not new with the coming of Jesus or with the writing of NT literature. Jesus is claiming that these were already central in the Old Testament. The evidence is abundant. For example, the prophet Micah said: "He has shown you, O mortal, what is good. And what does the LORD require of you? To act justly and to love mercy and to walk humbly with your God" (Micah 6:8).

We must remind ourselves that law does not mean a long list of dos and don'ts. Law (*tôrâ*) literally means "teaching," and the goal of the teaching is always to help foster right relationships with God and fellow human beings. In assessing how the law applies today, this must always be considered.

Notwithstanding all this, it is not always clear which OT commandments and prohibitions directly apply to us in current situations. The most basic guideline would seem to be whether a particular aspect of the law still promotes and helps facilitate the central concerns of the law: our relationship with God and with our fellow human beings.

We must always look to Jesus, for Jesus came precisely so that the law might be fulfilled. In some cases, "fulfilling" meant bringing a particular aspect of the law to completion by reaching its goal. In many cases, Jesus "fulfilled" the law by demonstrating in his own perfect obedience what was implied in keeping the law, thus showing the way and inviting us to follow. Jesus "fulfilled" the law by interpreting its true function and meaning for his followers. This is apparent in Matthew 5, where Jesus turned his attention away from strict literal adherence to the letter of the law and placed the focus on the heart of the matter, the heart of God, and the hearts of those who aim to please God by following Jesus' approach to law.

The law remains God's word, even when some parts of it are not literally applicable to us. Bible scholar Douglas Stuart says it well: "All of the Old Testament law is still the Word of God *for* us even though it is not still the command of God *to* us."[2]

## MESSENGERS OF RIGHTEOUSNESS

We often speak of the major prophets (Isaiah, Jeremiah, Ezekiel) and of the minor prophets (the rest). This division speaks to the length of the books that they wrote, but not necessarily to their relative importance. All the prophetic literature is important, as are narratives about prophets who did not leave behind written messages (including Elijah and Elisha). In our English Bible translations (following the Septuagint), the Minor Prophets include thirteen books. The Hebrew Bible combined all these except Daniel into one book, the Book of the Twelve. Daniel was not included with the prophetic literature, but rather with the Writings.

The prophetic books of the Hebrew canon included several books that we usually call historical books (Joshua, Judges, 1–2 Samuel, and 1–2 Kings). We call them historical books because they narrate historical events involving or affecting Israel. But they do more. They interpret and evaluate that history, showing how God is revealed in history, how God intervened in Israel's affairs, and how God used historical developments to further divine purposes. Thus, it is appropriate to treat these books as prophetic.

Many readers of Scripture assume that the prophetic books are mostly concerned with predicting the future, either the near future for Israel (for example, predictions of the coming Messiah) or the distant future (future even to us, including anticipated events at the end of time). It is easy, however, to misuse these books if we are overly preoccupied with a search in them for clues about our own and the world's future. Douglas Stuart maintains that less than 2 percent of OT prophecy speaks of the coming of a "Messiah," that less than 5 percent speaks of a future age where God's purposes are fulfilled, and that less than 1 percent deals with issues that have yet to be fulfilled—that is, speaks to aspects of *our* future.[3]

When the prophets reference future events, they usually speak of things in Israel's immediate future. But it is not as though these prophets were regularly given "inside information" to peer into the future and see in advance what was destined to happen. The prophets were not fortune tellers. They were teachers and proclaimers who understood the nature and the demands of the covenant. God called them to announce to Israel the consequences of Israel's spiritual and ethical behavior. God sometimes revealed to Israel through the prophets the specific nature of the positive or negative outcomes. But quite often the prophetic oracles were more general statements of the inevitable consequences of Israel's faithfulness and unfaithfulness.

Though the prophets sometimes spoke words directly revealed by God, sometimes they simply preached righteousness. They addressed ethical, religious, and political concerns from God's perspective. Peter describes it like this: "Prophets, though human, spoke from God as they were carried along by the Holy Spirit" (2 Peter 1:21). They knew how God had worked with Israel in the past. They knew what was contained in the covenant that God had made with Israel. And sometimes it did not take much special revelation to know what was ahead if Israel continued along a particular path. So the prophets' primary calling was to summon Israel back to faithfulness, to be "preachers of righteousness" (as described in 2 Peter 2:5).

It is easy to misunderstand how prophecy works. It is not as though God is the master fortune teller, able to peer into the future even better than any human. Let me illustrate this and describe an alternative with an anecdote. Imagine I would tell my daughter, "If you faithfully practice your violin without complaining, then tomorrow after your lesson, I will take you out for ice cream." Suppose she practices without complaint and I turn in to the ice cream shop on the way home from her lesson. Do you suppose she would marvel, "How did you know?" Of course not. She would be grateful that I was serious and that I remembered.

My "prediction" the day before would not imply I was peering into the future and seeing what lay ahead. I made a promise. My follow-through on that promise the next day would not confirm my ability to prognosticate. Rather, it would be an example of promise-keeping.

God's "predictions" should be viewed in the same way. When things happen just as God said they would, our response should not be, "God has an amazing ability to predict the future!" It should be, "When God speaks, God really is serious. God follows through on the consequences that have been spelled out in advance." When the consequences are negative, we should respond, "God really is serious about bringing us back to faithfulness." When the consequences are positive, we should respond, "God is a faithful God, showering us with blessings beyond what we could ever deserve."

Many who read the prophetic books find it difficult to make heads or tails of some texts. In my experience, historical context is particularly important when reading prophetic books, perhaps more so than for other OT books. For this we should seek the help of a study Bible or other reference tools. When we have a fair grasp of the historical situations being addressed, the texts themselves communicate much more clearly. Knowing where a specific prophetic oracle begins and ends can be helpful. Careful attention to paragraph divisions is crucial, for the prophetic books are mostly collections of discrete prophetic speeches.

The most important assignment of the prophets was to speak to their own contemporaries, not to speak to us. We can better discern what their messages mean for us if we interpret them in terms of their original meanings for Israel. Prophets helped Israel understand what God had done, what God was doing, and what God would still do. They used many forms of address—promises, woe oracles, legal disputes, judgment speeches, and so on—to facilitate covenant faithfulness. They challenged Israel to trust in God for their security, not rely on human diplomatic and military strategies. They called Israel to love and serve God with their whole hearts, not merely to practice religious ceremonies. And they insisted that what mattered most to God was to honor God above all and to treat both their fellow Israelites and the foreigners among them in ways consistent with God's justice and shalom. Here is a representative text:

> I hate, I despise your religious festivals;
>> your assemblies are a stench to me.
> Even though you bring me burnt offerings and grain offerings,
>> I will not accept them.
> Though you bring choice fellowship offerings,
>> I will have no regard for them.
> Away with the noise of your songs!
>> I will not listen to the music of your harps.
> But let justice roll on like a river,
>> righteousness like a never-failing stream!
> (Amos 5:21–24)

Prophetic words like this speak directly to our situations as well. Though the prophetic messages for today are not always as directly applicable as this one, we can discern in the prophetic books of the OT announcements of God's will and desires, revelations of God's nature and priorities, and glimpses of what God aims yet to accomplish in the life of Israel. By "Israel" I mean the set-apart people of God that has now been expanded with the coming of God's Spirit and the grafting into Israel of people from all cultures and nations—that is, the church. God's ancient prophets still speak to the ongoing work of God in the church and in the world.

## WISDOM AND WORSHIP

Many OT books were simply called "Writings" or sometimes "Psalms" by the Hebrews. We sometimes call these books wisdom literature. Most of them can be described as literary works of art: poetry, drama, lyrics of songs, and so on. The specific books that we usually put in this category are Job (a "historical drama"), Psalms (mostly a songbook), Proverbs, Ecclesiastes, and Song of Songs. As stated earlier, the Hebrews included other books that we might rather call history books (Ruth, Esther, the books of Chronicles) and one that we typically call prophecy (Daniel).

The psalms take center stage in this category of OT literature, and the whole collection is often named after them. This collection of 150 individual psalms contains thanksgiving hymns, praise songs, laments, and more. All had a place within Israel's worship. The whole range of human emotions finds expression in the picture language and the poetic expressions of these diverse psalms. Some speak for God, some about God, some to God. A conversation both *with* God and *about* God is often carried out within a single psalm. For these and many other reasons, psalms have always been highly valued in the church. Martin Luther claimed that in the Psalms we look right into the heart of all the saints. Dietrich Bonhoeffer maintained that in the Psalms we have an experience of exactly what Jesus also provides: We experience human words addressed to God and at the same time God's word addressed to us.

When and where were the psalms composed? There is no simple answer. We cannot always be sure that the psalms were really written by the people to whom they were later ascribed. But it is not unlikely that some came from the pen of Moses, about 1,450 years before Christ. The latest were likely written at least one thousand years later by anonymous authors after Israel's return from exile. Many were composed by David, Israel's great king and musician, and these can be dated to about the tenth century before Christ. Various collections of psalms finally found their way into one large collection, and since then have been passed on that way so that future generations can join Israel at worship, recall Israel's history, and enter into the presence of Israel's God. Thus it is appropriate for us to embrace this collection as our own as well, for we have joined Israel in its worship of this God; we have been adopted into the history of God's chosen people. These are our songs.

As the psalm collection grew, so did other collections of Jewish literature. The book of Job asks the ever-challenging questions: Is life fair? If not, why not? Why does God permit disease and catastrophe? Why do those who model faithfulness suffer these, sometimes as much as or more than the wicked? At the end of the book, God's voice speaks directly into the dramatic plotline, making the case that "God has set up the cosmos in a complex order well beyond Job's comprehension, and yet not beyond his appreciation. God knows a lot more than Job does, and yet what Job does see and understand of this catalog is beautiful, orderly, reassuring. So Job can trust God after all."[4]

The book of Proverbs, with many of its texts attributed to King Solomon, is really a collection of popular wisdom. Proverbs do not guarantee that a specific outcome always follows a given course of action. Rather, proverbs teach us to be wise, helping us discern which consequences are likely if we pursue a particular path.

Then there are the books of Ecclesiastes, Song of Songs, and Lamentations. They address human experiences of many kinds. There are struggles with meaninglessness and disorientation, passionate expressions of love, and despairing cries of hopelessness. These books do more than express human emotions. They also challenge and inspire us to think deeply about a range of theological and practical questions. God speaks also through these books and reveals to us a divine wisdom which centuries later is embodied in the person of Jesus, the Wisdom of God come in the flesh.

How exactly do these texts speak into our lives today? Psalms are regularly sung or read in our worship gatherings, and surely that is also the most appropriate place for them. It is entirely appropriate to read the psalms for personal devotional challenge and encouragement, though they were probably not composed primarily for this purpose. Their message resonates best when *we*, as a *community* of believers, use them to express our corporate worship to God.

An overly literal reading of poetic literature can get us into trouble. Some readers assume that each proverb represents a guarantee from God. This can hardly be the case, though, for it is not uncommon to see two proverbs next to each other that express a paradox (two different perspectives on the same issue). Take, for example, Proverbs 26:4: "Do not answer a fool according to his folly, or you yourself will be just like him." That sounds like clear instruction on how to respond to fools and the consequences of not doing it right. But consider the following proverb: "Answer a fool according to his folly, or he will be wise in his own eyes" (26:5). The truth is that sometimes the first proverb applies and sometimes the second. And that is how it usually is with proverbial statements. Wisdom consists in rightly discerning when one approach is the right one or, conversely, when the other one is.

James counsels: "If any of you lacks wisdom, you should ask God, who gives generously to all without finding fault, and it will be given to you" (James 1:5). Ultimately, God is the source of wisdom. The literal application of a long list of proverbs is not. And God gladly gives us the gift of wisdom, as we are told within the wisdom literature itself: "To the person who pleases him, God gives wisdom, knowledge and happiness" (Ecclesiastes 2:26).

The Song of Songs is a love song, and includes rather suggestive language for sexual expression of human love. It seems that the ancient Hebrews were less prudish about such descriptions than many Christians throughout church history have been. Many Christian interpreters claim that this book is about the relationship between God and Israel (or between Jesus and the church). I disagree. Even if it were, such a symbolic interpretation would make sense only if one first assumed that the love relationship portrayed in this literary work is the kind of relation that God wants humans to celebrate and enjoy in God-intended contexts.

It would take too much space to address every type of literature in the Old Testament in detail. But it is interesting to observe what the resurrected Jesus said: "Everything must be fulfilled that is written about me in the Law of Moses, the Prophets and the Psalms" (Luke 24:44). Even the wisdom literature finds its fulfillment in the life, death, and resurrection of Jesus. One finds in these texts predictions of the coming King and Redeemer. And when Jesus arrives, he shows us, just as these OT books do, what it means for a faithful Israelite to worship Israel's God, and what it means for the faithful God of Israel to stand by the chosen people. Just as Jesus is both human and divine, so are the words of these books both human words spoken to and about God and God's Word that continues to speak to us. Jesus fulfills what the wisdom literature aimed to do: demonstrate a relationship of true covenant faithfulness between God and Israel.

## WHY SHOULD WE READ AND SEEK TO UNDERSTAND THE OLD TESTAMENT?

The Old Testament contains countless treasures waiting to be discovered by the attentive reader. The greatest treasure of all is the wonderful portrait painted there, a picture that gradually unfolds from the first book to the last of a glorious creation and a chosen people experiencing the protection, the loving care, and the wise leadership of a faithful and gracious God who will bring all things to their intended destiny. And that picture was not finished by the time the Old Testament reached its final pages, nor was it with the completion of the New Testament, nor is it today. God is still at work, finishing the portrait, enacting the drama, creating something new. So many images can be used to remind us that God is not finished with this great creation project. But God will be faithful until that day when the final "It is finished!" will resound.

# Questions for discussion

---

1.  The Bible of the ancient Hebrews had three parts, none of which was called "history books." How does that influence our approach to OT books normally categorized as such?

2.  The main role of the prophets was not to predict the future, but to call Israel to faithful covenant living. How does that happen today?

3.  "The Old Testament contains countless treasures waiting to be discovered by the attentive reader. The greatest treasure of all is the wonderful portrait painted there, a picture that gradually unfolds from the first book to the last of a glorious creation and a chosen people experiencing the protection, the loving care, and the wise leadership of a faithful and gracious God who will bring all things to their intended destiny." How has this study of the Old Testament encouraged you to seek the hidden treasures contained within it?

# CONTINUING THE STORY IN THE NEW TESTAMENT

*[Jesus] began by saying to them, "Today this scripture is fulfilled in your hearing." —Luke 4:21*

At the beginning of Jesus' ministry, he presented himself as the one in whom and through whom the ancient promises were being fulfilled. We know from the New Testament that some OT promises, as well as some new promises made by Jesus during his life on earth, still await a future final fulfillment. The New Testament is the continuation of the OT story, but not its conclusion. Jesus and his first followers teach us how to read the Old Testament as the beginning—but only the beginning—of the grand story in which Jesus stands at the center.

❖

We have explored how Christians can benefit from appropriate attention to the Old Testament, indeed why they really cannot do without it. In this final chapter, we will work out some of the implications of what has been said for our reading of the New Testament.

Many Christians open their Bibles and almost by reflex start about three-fourths of the way through the book, as though the Old Testament did not even exist. They read the New Testament as though this part alone is "their" Bible. This happens either because someone has convinced them that the Old Testament is someone else's Bible or because they don't have clear ideas what to do with it. It is called "Old" and treated as if it were obsolete. I suppose no Christian ever completely dispenses with the Old Testament; it supplies some necessary background information for the New Testament and is therefore sometimes consulted for historical reasons. Most Christians are also aware that it contains prophetic statements concerning things that come to fulfillment in the NT era, so some consult the Old Testament to find these. There are helpful devotional passages here and there, especially in the Psalms. But that is about it. At best the Old Testament is viewed as a precursor to the New; at worst it is ignored.

Perhaps we must fully appreciate this: What we call the Old Testament was *the Bible*, the *whole* Bible, for Jesus, for the apostles, and for the earliest church. There is no evidence from the earliest decades of the Christian church that anyone ever expected any additional books would be added to their canon of Scripture. For them the Law, the Prophets, and the Writings were quite simply the Holy Scriptures (see Romans 1:2; 2 Timothy 3:15). As time passed, various additional books were written, in due course collected, and much later authorized as additional scripture. But these new books were neither written nor authorized as a *replacement* for OT scripture; they were authorized to supplement a canon fully accepted by the Christian church.

In time, Christians called the two separate collections the Old Testament and the New Testament. *Testament* is another word for *covenant*. Some Christians today refer to the Old Testament as the Hebrew Bible and the New Testament as the Christian Scriptures instead of the Old and New Testaments. Whatever we call them, in the first large part of our Bible we learn all about the covenant that God made with Israel, and in the Christian additions to it we see how that covenant was fulfilled and renewed and carried forward with the coming of Jesus and the new things that God did after Jesus died and rose and then sent the Spirit to live within and among God's people.

This covenant is new in many ways, though still building on what went before. First, the people of God were renewed in faithfulness, not merely by returning to faithful adherence to the older covenant, but through their allegiance to Jesus. Second, the law was written on human hearts as God had promised (Jeremiah 31:33). Third, the prophetic hope was now fulfilled that God's Spirit would empower not only select leaders of God's people but every constituent member (Joel 2:28–29). Fourth, just as God had always planned, God's "nation" was now being expanded to encompass representatives of all people groups. And these new believers could belong to Israel's God (and God's Israel; see Galatians 6:16) without first becoming ethnically or culturally Jewish. And all that was possible because God came to dwell among us in the person of God's only begotten Son, Jesus.

The New Testament thus continues and supplements what the Old Testament reports and promises. And the two components together now constitute the Bible that God has entrusted to the church.

## EXTENDING THE SALVATION HISTORY OF THE OLD TESTAMENT

We learn through the New Testament that forgiveness of sin and reconciliation with God have been made possible through the death and resurrection of Jesus Christ. But what does that imply about those who lived in earlier times? Did they not experience real forgiveness? The Old Testament repeatedly affirms that they did. They truly experienced God's forgiveness and were granted the privilege of living in a reconciled relationship with God, even though their lives preceded the life of Jesus, the one who came to enable that forgiveness and effect that reconciliation.

In ancient times, God had prescribed a system of sacrifices. Some of these were designed to facilitate acts of repentance and God's response, gracious forgiveness. When Israelites brought their animals or birds to the tabernacle or the temple to be slaughtered in God's presence, they were symbolizing and participating in deeper realities than mere animal-killing. They were bringing themselves in repentance to God and seeking God's graciously offered salvation. We should not reduce these activities to *mere symbols*. God received sinners and extended forgiveness and reconciliation in those contexts. In the light of the final sacrifice accomplished through Jesus, we are now invited to receive God's forgiveness through an act of faith, unaccompanied by the ancient sacrificial rituals.

In the light of the New Testament, we can see that the offerings prescribed in the Old Testament were more than just the rituals by which individuals were reconciled to God. They were also pointers toward the final sacrifice for sin in the death of Jesus (Romans 3:25). It is as though God extended forgiveness *in advance*, even though that forgiveness is ultimately considered a consequence of what had not yet been accomplished. In OT times, the Israelites looked forward to a coming Redeemer (and if they were not conscious that this is what they were doing, their sacrifices did it for them!). On the basis of the trusting faith that this represented, God truly forgave and accepted them. We now look backward in time as we place our faith in the Christ who died and rose again for our salvation.

The saints of old lived in a reconciled relationship with God, yet they did not experience everything that God promised them and us. The writer to the Hebrews formulates it like this: "All these people were still living by faith when they died. They did not receive the things promised; they only saw them and welcomed them from a distance, admitting that they were foreigners and strangers on earth" (Hebrews 11:13).

The ongoing story in which they lived and died continued in the New Testament. The promised Redeemer came and won salvation for the saints of old and for us. Through the Holy Spirit, God now writes the law upon our hearts. All are endowed with God's Spirit and are gifted to participate in ministry to one another and in the world. The kingdom has been established and the people of the covenant have been expanded to encompass representatives of all the peoples of the earth. Salvation history, begun in the Old Testament, is brought to completion in the New.

## EXPANDING THE OT PEOPLE OF GOD

Here is a short reminder of God's plan for God's people. In OT times, God brought into existence a new people group. God led, accompanied, protected, and sustained this people group through good times and bad. This ethnic people group eventually became a great nation. But God wanted more than that: God wanted a people of *faith*, so God established a covenant with Israel. Within this covenant, Israel experienced salvation. Israel was called to live out God's intentions for all humankind, openly before the watching world. Others would see, be amazed, and be drawn to follow the God of Israel.

Unfortunately, Israel was not always faithful, not always a model for others, and not always effective at drawing others to their God. But God never gave up on Israel; God remained faithful to the covenant. God promised that one day, Israel would be brought back to faithfulness so that God's intentions for Israel could be realized.

The New Testament tells us how God fulfilled that promise. Through John the Baptist at first, and then more fully through Jesus Christ, the call went forth: "The time has come. The kingdom of God has come near. Repent and believe the good news!" (Mark 1:15). Jesus' followers represented the renewed people of God. First through Jesus and then through his apostles, first to the Jews and then also to the Gentiles, the good news was made known. The OT people of God were fulfilling their calling.

Not all Jews embraced this. The Jews became a divided ethnic, national, and religious people. Some believed in Jesus; others rejected their promised Messiah. Those convinced joined the Jesus movement. Those not convinced ignored or opposed it. Jesus himself commented on the situation: "I say to you that many will come from the east and the west, and will take their places at the feast with Abraham, Isaac and Jacob in the kingdom of heaven. But the subjects of the kingdom will be thrown outside, into the darkness, where there will be weeping and gnashing of teeth" (Matthew 8:11–12).

Those Jews who rejected Jesus and continued to hope for a coming Savior remained outside the new covenant community. What God will yet do with and for those Jews is in God's hands. Gentiles who came to faith joined those in Israel confessing Jesus as Savior and Lord, and together these constitute the body of Christ, the church, the continuation of God's covenant people. We have inherited the ancient mission of Israel to be a light on the hill so that others will see the light of God and be drawn to faith (Matthew 5:14). Thus, God's new covenant people grows to encompass all the nations on earth (Revelation 5:9).

## BROADENING THE OT MISSION MANDATE

It was already clear in the Old Testament that people without a Jewish heritage or connection were welcome to join the people of God and were drawn by Israel's witness to the one true God. We find specific examples at various points in OT history, including the stories of Rahab, Ruth, and Naaman. The hope of the prophets was that one day there would be an unending stream of peoples making their way to Jerusalem, not to visit, but to become part of the people of God.

> In the last days
>> the mountain of the LORD's temple will be established
>>> as the highest of the mountains;
>> it will be exalted above the hills,
>>> and all nations will stream to it.
>
> Many peoples will come and say,
>> "Come, let us go up to the mountain of the LORD,
>>> to the temple of the God of Jacob.
>> He will teach us his ways,
>>> so that we may walk in his paths."
>> The law will go out from Zion,
>>> the word of the LORD from Jerusalem.
>> (Isaiah 2:2–3)

Scholar Gerhard Lohfink describes it like this: "The Gentiles, fascinated by the salvation visible in Israel, are driven of their own accord to the people of God. They do not become believers as a result of missionary activity; rather, the fascination emitted by the people of God draws them close."[1]

We have already quoted Jesus' main message: "The time has come. The kingdom of God has come near" (Mark 1:15). Jesus announced that the time of waiting was over. God's plan would move forward even if not everyone in Israel was ready to join. Those who were ready to receive the kingdom and press on with the mission would now become the nucleus of the renewed people of God. The great pilgrimage of the nations began with Jesus' ministry, sometimes with a small trickle and sometimes with a cascade of people saying yes to Jesus and his message.

Jesus designated twelve of his followers to be a special core group that would be sent out to spread the good news. These twelve stood symbolically for the twelve tribes of Israel, as they now constituted the true people of God. They were now newly commissioned by Jesus to be the light on the hill (Matthew 5:14). Their final commission is well known: "All authority in heaven and on earth has been given to me. Therefore go and make disciples of all nations, baptizing them in the name of the Father and of the Son and of the Holy Spirit, and teaching them to obey everything I have commanded you. And surely I am with you always, to the very end of the age" (28:18–20).

Note two major changes: First, the commission to bring God's blessing to the whole world is no longer the task of "all Israel" (understood ethnically and nationally), but rather the task of that part of Israel ready to recognize Jesus as Lord and Messiah. These who hear Christ's commission to be that visible and audible missionary force will draw others to faith.

Second, the mission mandate to draw Gentiles to faith in the God of Israel is no longer viewed as a movement of *passively attracting* others to come. In the Old Testament, the initiative often lay with the outlying nations. They would see, they would be fascinated, and they would come. Now the initiative must come from Jesus' followers as they go out into all the world and invite people of every nation to join the one true people of God.

Rest assured, the movement *outward* to all the world does not erase the other side of the coin. God still wants to use the people of God to *draw people in*. The church of Jesus Christ is called to live before the watching world in such a way that others are drawn to faith. The attraction of the gospel should be irresistible. In that sense, the church in every location is a new temple to which others will be drawn. In every location, God takes up residence in the local gathering of the covenant people. In every location, the word of God goes forth, people are drawn to faith, and they join the growing people of God.

The church in all places is called to be the light on the hill, drawing attention to the one true God who invites all to experience salvation.

## SUPPLEMENTING THE OT PORTRAITS OF GOD

Jesus once said to his disciples, "Do not be afraid, little flock, for your Father has been pleased to give you the kingdom" (Luke 12:32). Note the portraits of God in this one short verse. If we are God's flock, then God is a shepherd. Yet God is called a father here, implying that we are God's children. Yet because God's kingdom is being given to us, God is also a king. In one short sentence, Jesus combines three of the main images of God in the Old Testament: shepherd, parent, and king.

In the New Testament, Jesus claims for himself virtually all the key titles of God in the Old Testament. He calls himself

"I am" (John 8:58), taking up the name for God in the Old Testament, Yahweh. Jesus is also the good shepherd (John 10:11), and Jesus is called Immanuel (God with us; Matthew 1:23). Jesus presents himself as more than a rabbi, more than a prophet, more even than the Messiah, the promised Savior: in Jesus, God came to be present on earth in human form.

Not everyone who saw him recognized this fact. Often, the disciples themselves did not grasp the point. Yet the gospel writers and the Christian church after them declared: Jesus is truly a human person; but just as truly, Jesus is God. As a human, Jesus shows us how to trust our Shepherd, our Parent, our King. As God, Jesus fills out the OT pictures, making God's work among us visible. He does it by calming storms, by praying for us, by "passing by" and by speaking out "I am" in our presence. Those who know the Old Testament see in Jesus the one who brings Israel's God near to us and shows us what God is like.

Jesus also fills out the portrait of the OT warrior God. In OT times, Israel's God did indeed sometimes fight for and with Israel as they took up weapons and defeated powerful enemies. In Jesus, something new began. God came to be among us, not to fight for God's people against human enemies, but to love even enemies and to save them too. Because in Christ God died for us while we were still God's enemies (see Romans 5:10), we are now called to love our enemies and if necessary to die at their hands rather than kill them with ours.

We now recognize who the real enemies are and why we need weapons more powerful than any military machinery: "For our struggle is not against flesh and blood, but against the rulers, against the authorities, against the powers of this dark world and against the spiritual forces of evil in the heavenly realms" (Ephesians 6:12). The victories we win are described like this:

Now have come the salvation and the power
   and the kingdom of our God,
   and the authority of his Messiah.
For the accuser of our brothers and sisters,
   who accuses them before our God day and night,
   has been hurled down.
They triumphed over him
   by the blood of the Lamb
   and by the word of their testimony;
they did not love their lives so much
   as to shrink from death.
(Revelation 12:10–11)

The same God who in the Old Testament often rescued Israel through military victories now wins the decisive battle over the real and final enemy, wins it through love, faithfulness, and self-sacrifice, embodied and enacted through Jesus Christ and his death on the cross. We are privileged to participate in this victory by laying down earthly weapons ourselves, following Jesus, and giving our lives for a cause that cannot fail.

## RENEWING THE OT HOPE

The Old Testament ends with eyes strained toward the future. God had done great things, but greater things were up ahead. Wonderful promises were not yet fulfilled. When Jesus stepped onto the scene, he announced that the time of fulfillment had arrived. God's reign was being established.

But the New Testament also ends with eyes strained toward the future. Many promises made to ancient Israel and many to the apostles and the NT church still await fulfillment. God's reign has begun but has not yet been consummated. It is *already*, and it is also *not yet*. Just as faithful Israelites in ancient times looked forward in hope to the day when God would bring history to its goal in a renewed heaven and earth, so also do we.

The New Testament continues the story begun in the Old Testament. Someday that story will reach its final chapter. It will do so not by adding chapters to a biblical book, or books to the canon of Scripture. It will do so by fulfilling a story still in progress. All humanity is invited to be a part of that story. It began in Genesis 1, continued through Revelation 22, and reaches its goal as we live into and out of this story, faithfully and joyfully living and proclaiming it in our lives, our Christian communities, and our world, until Jesus is all in all.

# *Questions for discussion*

1. "In the light of the New Testament, we can see that the offerings prescribed in the Old Testament were more than just the rituals by which individuals were reconciled to God. They were also pointers toward the final sacrifice for sin in the death of Jesus. It is as though God extended forgiveness *in advance*, even though that forgiveness is ultimately to be viewed as a consequence of what had not yet been accomplished." That is one example of reading the Old Testament with eyes trained by the New Testament. What other examples of this come to mind?

2. "Those Jews who rejected Jesus and continued to hope for a coming Savior remained outside the new covenant community. What God will yet do with and for these is something best left in God's hands." How do you respond to this claim?

3. What is your response to the grand story of Scripture, from creation to consummation? Does it raise challenging questions? Does it inspire you to pursue greater faithfulness? Does it fill you with hope?

# ACKNOWLEDGMENTS

*Seminary colleagues and administrators:* I wrote this book during the year I officially retired from the teaching position that was my primary calling for almost my entire adult life. I graduated from Mennonite Brethren Biblical Seminary (now Fresno Pacific University Biblical Seminary) in 1978, and when I came back to teach in 1986, most of my former professors became my colleagues. Throughout the decades, my colleagues have been my friends. School administrators have generously provided permission and encouragement to take leaves of absence to Germany and to undertake ministry trips to countries far and wide. They have also freed me to write books and to serve my own denomination in Canada and the United States. The friends and colleagues I have learned to know and love in all these places have enriched my life and ministry. Thank you to all of you.

*Editors and publishers:* Various publishers have taken a chance on me. These include Sheffield Academic Press, which published my revised doctoral dissertation; Kindred Press, which published several books interpreting Scripture; Faith & Life Press, which often encouraged me to write Bible study guides;

and Herald Press, which published my Mark commentary, my ethics book, and now this guidebook in reading the Old Testament. And then there are my German collaborators and publishers. Thank you to Kurt Kerber, to Dr. Ulrich Wendel, and to others for giving me multiple opportunities to write for yearbooks, magazines, and study Bibles. Thank you especially to David Neufeld, who has been my publishing companion ever since the start of Neufeld Verlag. I thank you all, and now specifically the incredible editors at Herald Press for helping bring this book to birth.

*My family:* I begin with my family of origin. I am grateful that my dad taught me to pay attention to English grammar, besides all the other things he taught me about the Bible and about life. I thank Mom for teaching me to take on challenges and stick with them to the end, and for unending support for our family and for me personally. You continue to be a huge inspiration.

And I have nothing but gratitude for my own wonderful, large, blended family. Thanks, Gertrud, for being there all along the way, and for inspiring and challenging me every time I took on another writing project. Thanks, all my children, for sacrifices you've made along the way as your dad sometimes worked overtime and often traveled. You've been amazing. Special thanks, Eliana, for joining our family so late, and for being the best young friend an older daddy could ever imagine.

# NOTES

## CHAPTER 1

1. Thomas R. Shepherd, ed., *The Genesis Creation Account and Its Reverberations in the New Testament* (Berrien Springs, MI: Andrews University Press, 2022), 24.
2. John Dominic Crossan and Richard G. Watts, *Who Is Jesus? Answers to Your Questions about the Historical Jesus* (Louisville: Westminster John Knox Press, 1999).
3. See James B. Stump, ed., *Four Views on Creation, Evolution, and Intelligent Design* (Grand Rapids: Zondervan, 2017); and John Walton, *The Lost World of Genesis One: Ancient Cosmology and the Origins Debate* (Downers Grove, IL: InterVarsity Press, 2009).
4. Those who wish to explore these issues in greater depth are encouraged to check out the resources made available by BioLogos at BioLogos.org.

## CHAPTER 2

1. C. S. Lewis, *The Lion, the Witch, and the Wardrobe* (New York: HarperCollins, 1978), 179.

## CHAPTER 3

1. Bernhard Ott, *God's Shalom Project: An Engaging Look at the Bible's Sweeping Story* (Intercourse, PA: Good Books, 2004), 30–31.

## CHAPTER 4

1. See Bernhard Ott, *God's Shalom Project: An Engaging Look at the Bible's Sweeping Story* (Intercourse, PA: Good Books, 2004), 42.

## CHAPTER 5

1. See Bernhard Ott, *God's Shalom Project: An Engaging Look at the Bible's Sweeping Story* (Intercourse, PA: Good Books, 2004), 44.

## CHAPTER 6

1. See also my defense of this third alternative in Jon Isaak, ed., *The Old Testament and the Life of God's People* (University Park, PA: Eisenbrauns, 2009), 257–67.

## CHAPTER 7

1. Duane A. Garrett, *The Problem of the Old Testament: Hermeneutical, Schematic, and Theological Approaches* (Downers Grove, IL: InterVarsity, 2020), 16–17.

## CHAPTER 8

1. Wikipedia, s.v. "Attributes of God in Christianity," accessed March 1, 2023, https://en.wikipedia.org/wiki/Attributes_of_God_in_Christianity.
2. N. T. Wright, *Simply Jesus: Who He Was, What He Did, Why It Matters* (San Francisco: HarperOne, 2011), 58–59.
3. I draw this term from a public lecture delivered by Kenneth Bailey, First Armenian Presbyterian Church, Fresno, California, March 7, 2008.

## CHAPTER 9

1. Gott kann auch auf krummen Linien gerade Striche schreiben.
2. Millard Lind, *Yahweh Is a Warrior: The Theology of Warfare in Ancient Israel* (Scottdale, PA: Herald Press, 1986), 108.
3. Lind, 107.
4. See my interpretation of Acts 15 in *All Right Now: Finding Consensus on Ethical Questions* (Scottdale, PA: Herald Press, 2008), 187–99.

## CHAPTER 10

1. For a much more detailed interpretation of this very important chapter in Acts, see Timothy J. Geddert, *All Right Now: Finding Consensus on Ethical Questions* (Scottdale, PA: Herald Press, 2008), 187–99.
2. Gordon Fee and Douglas Stuart, *How to Read the Bible for All Its Worth* (Grand Rapids: Zondervan, 2003), 169.
3. Fee and Stuart, 182.
4. John Stackhouse, *Can God Be Trusted? Faith and the Challenge of Evil* (Oxford: Oxford University Press, 1998), 98.

## CHAPTER 11

1. Gerhard Lohfink, *Jesus and Community: The Social Dimensions of Christian Faith* (Philadelphia: Fortress, 1984), 19.

# SCRIPTURE INDEX

*Page numbers in italics indicate that the scripture reference appears multiple times on the same page.*

## OLD TESTAMENT

### Genesis

## Revelation

# THE AUTHOR

Timothy J. Geddert is professor emeritus of New Testament at Fresno Pacific Biblical Seminary in Fresno, California, where he has taught New Testament since 1986. He has a PhD in New Testament from Aberdeen University (Scotland). Tim has written books on biblical interpretation, ecclesiology, and ethics in English and in German. He  has also written commentaries on Mark and Luke and numerous Bible study books and booklets. Tim and his wife Gertrud have seven children.